Longing for a Kiss

LOVE POEMS FROM MANY LANDS

Longing for a Kiss

LOVE POEMS FROM MANY LANDS

COMPILED BY THE
EDITORS OF HIPPOCRENE BOOKS

HIPPOCRENE BOOKS
New York

Contents

❧ American Poems ☙

❧ Arabic Poems ☙

∞ Chinese Poems ∞

∞ Czech Poems ∞

∽ Egyptian Poem (Coptic) ∽

∽ English Poems ∽

∞ Finnish Poems ∞

∞ French Poems ∞

∽ German Poems ∽

∽ Greek Poems ∽

❧ Hungarian Poems ❧

❧ Indian Poems ❧

❧ Irish Poems ❧

∞ Italian Poems ∞

❦ Jewish Poems ❧

❦ Persian Poem ❧

❦ Polish Poems ❧

☙ Roman Poems ☙

☙ Russian Poems ☙

☙ Scottish Poems ☙

∞ Spanish Poems ∞

∞ Ukrainian Poems ∞

American Poems

"Spring in Central Park" by William Zorach, 1914.

EDGAR ALLAN POE (1809–1849)

A Dream Within a Dream

Take this kiss upon the brow!
And, in parting from you now,
Thus much let me avow—
You are not wrong, who deem
That my days have been a dream:
Yet if hope has flown away
In a night, or in a day,
In a vision, or in none,
Is it therefore the less *gone*?
All that we see or seem
Is but a dream within a dream.

I stand amid the roar
Of a surf-tormented shore,
And I hold within my hand
Grains of the golden sand—
How few! yet how they creep
Through my fingers to the deep,
While I weep—while I weep!
O God! can I not grasp
Them with a tighter clasp?
O God! can I not save
One from the pitiless wave?
Is *all* that we see or seem
But a dream within a dream?

PAUL LAURENCE DUNBAR (1872–1906)

A Negro Love Song

Seen my lady home las' night,
　　Jump back honey, jump back.
Hel' huh han' an' sque'z it tight,
　　Jump back honey, jump back.
Heahd huh sigh a little sigh,
Seen a light gleam f'um huh eye,
An' a smile go flitin' by—
　　Jump back honey, jump back.

Heahd de win' blow thoo de pines,
　　Jump back honey, jump back.
Mockin' bird was singin, fine,
　　Jump back honey, jump back.
An' my hea't was beatin' so,
When I reached my lady's do',
Dat I couldn't ba' to go—
　　Jump back, honey, jump back.

Put my ahm aroun' huh wais',
　　Jump back, honey, jump back.
Raised huh lips an took a tase',
　　Jump back, honey, jump back.
Love me honey, love me true?
Love me well ez I love you?
An' she ansawhd: "'Cose I do"—
　　Jump back, honey, jump back.

SARA TEASDALE (1884–1933)

The Look

Strephon kissed me in the spring,
  Robin in the fall,
But Colin only looked at me
  And never kissed at all.

Strephon's kiss was lost in jest,
  Robin's lost in play,
But the kiss in Colin's eyes
  Haunts me night and day.

SARA TEASDALE (1884–1933)

The Kiss

Before you kissed me only winds of heaven
Had kissed me, and the tenderness of rain—
Now you have come, how can I care for kisses
Like theirs again?

I sought the sea, she sent her winds to meet me,
They surged about me singing of the south—
I turned my head away to keep still holy
Your kiss upon my mouth.

And swift sweet rains of shining April weather
Found not my lips where living kisses are;
I bowed my head lest they put out my glory
As rain puts out a star.

I am my love's and he is mine forever,
Sealed with a seal and safe forevermore—
Think you that I could let a beggar enter
Where a king stood before?

F. SCOTT FITZGERALD (1896–1940)

My First Love

All my ways she wove of light
   Wove them half alive,
Made them warm and beauty-bright . . .
   So the shining, ambient air
Clothes the golden waters where
   The pearl fishers dive.

When she wept and begged a kiss
   Very close I'd hold her,
Oh I know so well in this
   Fine, fierce joy of memory
She was very young like me
   Tho' half an aeon older.

Once she kissed me very long,
   Tip-toed out the door,
Left me, took her light along,
   Faded as a music fades . . .
   Then I saw the changing shades,
   Color-blind no more.

Arabic Poems

`ANTARAH (C. 590 A.D.)

From the Mu`allaqah of `Antarah

She takes your heart with the flash edge of her smile,
  her mouth sweet to the kiss, sweet to the taste,

As if a draft of musk from a spiceman's pouch
  announced to wet gleam of her inner teeth,

Or an untouched meadow, bloom and grass
  Sheltered in rain, untrodden, dung free, hidden.

Over it the white, first clouds of spring
  pour down, leaving small pools like silver dirhams,

Pouring and bursting, evening or evening
  gushing over it in an endless stream.

The fly has it all to himself, and is not about to leave,
  droning softly, like a wine drinker humming a tune,

Then buzzing elbow on elbow, like a one-armed man
  kindling a fire, bent down over the flint.

edited by Suzanne Pinckney Stetkevych

SA'ID AQL (B. 1912)

Samrà'u

Samara, O childhood dream,
Impregnable, miserly lips,
Approach me not, remain as
A thought of beauty for my morrow.

My heart is full of a sweet
Void; so enter it not.
I fear it would choke
Beneath your moist, perfumed kisses,
And vanish over the horizon
Through your kohl-anointed lashes.

What has beauty taken
From you and your plaited trees?
Its light? I would gladly die for the light
Born of your languid glance.
Your mouth replies to a smile:
"Go, paint the corpse's flowers."
The earth as you pass is an awakening
From the deep slumber of dream,
Joyous as if your flashing smile
Were some small chink of hope.

Samara, remain one among
The unattainable delights:
The object of my lip's desire
And of my distraught gaze:
That morrow for which we long
And death, stealing forward, grasps.

translated by Mounah Khouri and Hamid Algar

MUHAMMAD AL-FAYTURI (B. 1930)

To Two Unknown Eyes

Mistress . . .
Should these enamored words chance to meet your eyes
Or pass between your lips
Then forgive me; it was your eyes
In whose shade one evening I leaned resting
And snatched brief slumber
In their repose I caressed the stars and moon
I wove a boat of fancy out of petals
And laid down my tired soul
Gave to drink my thirsty lip
Quenched my eye's desire

Mistress . . .
When we met by chance as strangers meet
My sorrow too was walking on the road
Bare, unveiled
With heavy tread
You were my sorrow
Sadness and loss
silence and regret
Were embracing a poet consumed by struggle
For poetry, mistress, is a stranger in my land
Killed by emptiness and void
My spirit trembled when I saw you
I felt suddenly as if a dagger delved into my blood
Cleansed my heart, my mouth
Prostrated me with soiled brow and supplicating hands
In the shade of your sweet eyes

Mistress . . .
If suddenly we meet
If my eyes see those your eyes
High-set, green, drowned in mist and rain

If on the road by another chance we meet
And what is chance but fate?
Then would I kiss the road, kiss it twice.

translated by Mounah Khouri and Hamid Algar

Chinese Poems

HSÜ CHIH-MO (1895–1931)

A Night in Florence

You are really going tomorrow? Then I, I . . . well,
You don't have to bother, sooner or later there will be such
    a day.
If you wish to remember me, then remember,
Or else forget, while there's still time, that I ever
Existed in this world so you won't be sad in vain when you
    do recall.
Treat it as a dream, a fleeting hallucination;
Treat it as the withered blossoms we saw the day before
    yesterday
That trembled in the wind, shedding one petal,
Then another. On the ground they lay, trodden by someone
    into dust . . .
Ai, trodden by someone into dust—into dust, that'd be at least
    clean-cut,
It's really torture to be neither living nor dead, to look
So shabby, unwanted, and to be the object of slighting glances—
Heavens! Why should you do it, why should you do it. . . .
But I just cannot forget you. That day when you came,
It was like a ray of bright light in darkness.
You are my teacher, my love, and my savior.
You taught me what life is and what love is;
You brought me out of bewilderment back to my innocence;
Without you how could I ever know the sky is high and
    grass green?
Feel my heart, see how fast it beats this moment; and
Feel my cheeks, see how hot they burn; fortunately in the
    dark night
Nobody can see them. My love, I cannot even breathe now,
Kiss me no more, this life aflame I cannot bear.
My soul at this moment is a chunk of hot iron on an anvil,
Being struck by the hammer of love, again and again,
Its sparks flying in all directions . . . I feel faint, please hold me,

My love, just let me die in your embrace with my eyes closed
In this quiet garden—how beautiful it would be!
The sound of the wind in the birch trees above, rustling,
Rings out a dirge for me; the breeze having come
From an olive grove, brings over the scent of pomegranate
    blossoms,
And takes away my soul. There are also the fireflies,
Sentimental fireflies who light up the way for me
As I halt my steps on the three-arched bridge to listen
To your grief-stricken calls: you hold in your arms my body
That's still warm, hugging it, kissing it, and tightly enfolding
    it . . .
With a smile I follow the breeze on my way again,
Letting it lead me to heaven, or hell, or anywhere,
So long as I leave this loathed human life to realize death
In love. Isn't this death in the embrace of love better
Than five hundred reincarnations? . . . Selfish? Yes, I know,
But I cannot bother now . . . Are you going to die with me?
What? If we are not together, the death cannot be "death
    in love."
To soar to heaven requires two pairs of wings beating in unison,
And even in heaven we need each other's care.
I cannot go without you, nor you without me; if it is to hell
That I descend, you would like it less for me to go alone.
You said that Hades is not more civilized than this world
(Though I don't believe it): a fragile flower like me
Surely will face the ravage of winds and rains, and then
Much as I may call you, you cannot hear—
Wouldn't that be plunging into a mire instead of gaining
    salvation,
Letting the unfeeling ghosts together with heartless human beings
Ridicule my fate, ridicule your timid carelessness?
This, too, has reason. Well, what shall I do then?
It's so hard to live, and yet unfree even in death, not to say
I do not want you to sacrifice your future for my sake . . .
Ai, you said it's still better to live and wait, wait for that day!
Is there going to be that day?—So long as you live, my faith
    remains;

But you have to go at daybreak, can you really bear
To leave me behind? I cannot detain you, this is fate.
Only we know that when a flower is without sunshine or dew,
Its petals will turn yellow and dry so pitifully!
You cannot forget me, my love, only in your heart can I
Find my life; yes, I'll listen to you, and I'll wait,
Even if it is for the iron tree to bloom, still I'll wait;
My love, you are a star above me shining forever.
If perchance I die I will change myself into a firefly
Hovering low in this garden, near the grass,
From dusk till midnight, and from midnight till dawn.
My only hope is that no cloud will come over the sky
So I may gaze at the sky, at that unchanging star—at you.
My only wish is that you shine more brightly for me through
    the night
And across the sky to link the hearts of love together. . . .

SHAO HSÜN-MEI (B. 1903)

A Dream

The lovely, the terrible, and the proud
The tip of a virgin's tongue, the tip of a lizard's tail
I cannot understand; can you tell me,
Is there true happiness among four lips?

Ah, the rose-colored, the ivory-colored, a bed full,
This sweet dream keeps my soul on errand:
I am a loyal disciple of sin,
I want to see a worldly nun disrobe.

SHAO HSÜN-MEI (B. 1903)

May

Ah, lusty May is again burning,
A sin is born of a virgin's kiss;
Sweet tears tempt me, always tempt me
To feel between her breasts with my lips.

Here life is as eternal as death,
As the trembling happiness on a wedding night;
If she is not a rose, a rose all white,
Then she must be redder than the red of blood.

Ah, this firelike, and fleshlike
Darkness of light and tears of laughter
Are the soul of my love's soul
And the enemy to the enemy of my hate.

Heaven has just opened two large gates,
O God, I am not one to enter.
I have already found comfort in hell,
Already have I dreamed of an awakening in the short night.

Czech Poems

"The Kiss" by Constantin Brancusi, circa 1908.

ADOLF HEYDUK (1835–1923)

She Came to Me at Night

She came to me at night,
we stood in the orchard,
cocks in the villages
were loudly crowing,
on the sky were glowing
bright heavenly lights,
but she, like the sun,
bloomed in my heart.

She bloomed with a fiery gratitude,
blissful and smiling,
she embraced me with affection
like a dark vine-shoot
and when in blissful trembling
she pressed my head to her breasts
she whispered: "Ah, why does this night
not last three years?"

Three years is not enough,
I would have only grief,
too soon before I could kiss you all over
the dawn would flare up on the horizon.
If I should kiss thoroughly,
with gratitude for all your charms,
such a night, my fairy,
would have to last three hundred years.

JAROSLAV VRCHLICKÝ (1853–1912)

Music in the Soul

In a far corner of the human hearts,
there is a hidden music,
that rings there, talks and sings,
even if silenced for years, it sounds again at times,
especially, at quiet evenings of the summer night,
when all the strings of our heart are aroused
by that master of tones, the god of the universe, love.

I have often asked my heart: What is love?
And in answer, throughout the universe sounded music
that made my heart quiver in a secret joy:
Love is a bird that in the cage of the world is singing,
it likes to be quiet in day, bursts into singing at night,
always rejoicing, although in despair at times.

Love is a treasure not diminished by time;
a hive full of honey is love,
it is the smile of the day and the miracle of the night,
it is the most mysterious music of the starry skies,
it is a waterfall that in a far corner of the heart is singing,
it is the heart's world and it is the world's heart.

Oh, you weary, tired heart,
only have faith and a ray will shimmer at times,
even for you at the tree of life sings
the wondrous bird that is called love,
even for you is emerging the starry music
that is pouring out from your face, holy night!

I often wandered, lost my way in the quiet night
and asked: Earth, where beats your heart?
And asked: World, where is that mysterious music
that from the beginnings, sounds through space and time?
And everything around answered: Love, love,
with it all is standing, in everything it burns and sings.

I already cease to speak—but in the bushes the lark is singing
and the golden stars are hurrying through the fragrant night,
below the window in the shadows young love is whispering,
lips are silenced by a kiss and a beat of the heart,
and if a smile rings in the dusk at times,
it sounds like the music of starlings and doves.

You are the poetry, the *music* that *sings*
and flies throughout *time,* storm and *night,*
and guides the *heart* in which burns eternal *love!*

ANTONÍN SOVA (1864–1928)

Song

At home again after years
I took the violin into my hands!
So awkwardly, softly
trembled the timid sound!
Trembled the timid sound—
I have already forgotten how to play,
oh, in vain! I am remembering,
I have already forgotten how to play!

And in my desire and longing
for the soft violin of mine,
that wept so sadly
in the moonlit nights—
in the moonlit nights—!
I stroke the string harder,
oh, in vain, the string broke,
I have already forgotten how to play!

And she, who used to like
my ponderous talk,
did not even shudder,
her searching look did not glare!
Her searching look did not glare
after the years, how sad!
I grew old and long since
I have forgotten how to kiss!

VÍTĚZSLAV NEZVAL (1900–1958)

About the Beauties of the Female Body

Oh unending beauty of the body
that my love bestowed upon me!
When I gazed into her eyes
I thought that an angel came to me.
Her velvety mouth
that trembled when kissed!
I only say of her bosom that
it glistened and was exquisite.

No, I will not again encounter
a forehead so heavenly arched.
I used to enter into her mystery
piously, as into a cathedral.
When she said: Oh God, enough—,
only then the greatest was her desire.
As time went by I had forgotten her—,
and she also had forgotten me.

JAROSLAV SEIFERT (1901—1986)

Dialogue

(She) Were you kissing my forehead, or was it my lips?
I do not know,
—I only had heard the sweet voice,
and then the thick darkness
enveloped the wonder of my startled eyelids.

(He) I kissed you hurriedly on the forehead,
intoxicated
by the fragrance of your streaming breath,
and I do not know,

—I only had heard the sweet voice,
and then the thick darkness
enveloped the wonder of my startled eyelids.
Were you kissing my forehead, or was it my lips?

FRANTIŠEK NECHVÁTAL (1905–1983)

Fire

Your kisses are like touches of wings,
with them the heaviness is removed from our souls.
The touch changes into a light breeze, and
hovering above the breeze is an intoxicating mist.

Inside your beautiful body nests a dark sin,
and your coarse hair breathes with holy glow.
In dream lands I sing alone
for so many kind and sad souls.

In a blue dusk my dream sadly fades,
little streams of tenderness flow through your voice.
Someone close by, trembled between us
and thirst fused itself to the damp lips.

Fire and water from crystal fields
rush towards you with a devouring desire.
Solitude, heavy with wine, will quietly begin
a shy confession about its pain.

Like a fragrant morsel was burning your mouth,
mysterious woman, warm with sweet heat.
When two stars collide on their path
who will then, in terror, protect love from the fire?

FRANTIŠEK HRUBÍN (1910–1971)

Of this World

Now you are turning your head, it is aphelion.
You dim the glow of your hair with your palm.
I recognize you by the fragrance of your skin,
my remembrance is of this world.

If only the nights could be merciful again;
and my lips closed by kisses
will sail onto the wide sea of breath
into the quietness between your breasts.

Egyptian Poem

Love Spell to Horus

♀ I am . . .*child of . . .*
  I entered through a door of stone
I exited through a door of iron
I entered with my head down
I found seven maidens sitting by a spring.
I desired but they desired not,
I agreed but they agreed not.
I desired to love . . .*daughter of . . .*
But she desired not my kiss.
I strengthened myself and stood up.
I cried and sighed till the tears of my eyes
Soaked the soles of my feet.

       Isis: "What ails you, man, son or Re,
       Who cried and sighs till the tears of your eyes
       Soak the soles of your feet?"

       Horus: "Why, Isis, do you not wish me to cry?
       I entered through a door of stone,
       I exited through a door of iron.
       I entered with my head down,
       I exited with my feet down.
       I found seven maidens there by a spring.
       I desired but they desired not,
       I agreed but they agreed not.
       I desired to love . . .*daughter of . . .*
       But she desired not my kiss."

---

*Insert the relevant names of your intended here in place of the dots. This is an ancient spell based on the legend where Horus complains to his mother Isis that he has met seven maidens who have rejected his advances.

Isis: "Why did you enter by a door of stone
And exit by a door of iron,
And find seven maidens
And desire but they desired not,
And desire to love . . .*daughter of . . .*
But she refused your kiss?
No, you did not strengthen yourself nor stand up,
For you sent not forth seven tongues,
Saying THETE seven times!"

O Great One among the Spirits,
I desire that . . .*daughter of . . .*
Spend forty days and forty nights
Hanging on me like a bitch for a dog,
Like a sow for a boar.
For I am the one who calls
And you are the one who must love!

English Poems

"The Kiss" by Francesco Hayez, circa 1859.

SIR THOMAS WYATT (C. 1503–1542)

Remembrance

They flee from me, that sometime did me seek
  With naked foot, stalking in my chamber.
I have seen them gentle, tame, and meek,
  That now are wild, and do not remember
  That sometime they put themselves in danger
    To take bread at my hand; and now they range
    Busily seeking with a continual change.

Thanked for fortune it hath been otherwise
  Twenty times better; but once, in special,
In thin array, after a pleasant guise,
  When her loose gown from her shoulders did fall,
  And she me caught in her arms long and small,
    Therewith all sweetly did me kiss
    And softly said, 'Dear heart, how like you this?'

It was no dream; I lay broad waking:
  But all is turned, thorough my gentleness,
Into a strange fashion of forsaking;
  And I have leave to go of her goodness,
  And she also to use newfangleness.
    But since that I so kindly am served,
    I would fain know what she hath deserved.

SIR THOMAS WYATT (C. 1503–1542)

Alas! madam, for stealing of a kiss,
    Have I so much your mind then offended?
Have I then done so grievously amiss,
    That by no means it may be amended?
Then revenge you, and the next way is this:
    Another kiss shall have my life ended.
For to my mouth the first my heart did suck,
The next shall clean out of my breast it pluck.

"The First Kiss" by William Bouguereau, 1890.

JOHN LYLY (C. 1554–1606)

Cards and Kisses

Cupid and my Campaspe played
At cards for kisses, Cupid paid;
He stakes his quiver, bow, and arrows,
His mother's doves, and team of sparrows;
Loses them too; then, down he throws
The coral of his lip, the rose
Growing on's cheek (but none knows how);
With these, the crystal of his brow,
And then the dimple of his chin:
All these did my Campaspe win.
At last, he set her both his eyes;
She won, and Cupid blind did rise.
    O Love! has she done this to thee?
    What shall (alas!) become of me?

MICHAEL DRAYTON (1563–1631)

Sonnet

iv

Since there's no help, come let us kiss and part.
    Nay, I have done; you get no more of me,
And I am glad, yea, glad with all my heart,
    That thus so cleanly I myself can free;
Shake hands for ever, cancel all our vows,
    And when we meet at any time again,
Be it not seen in either of our brows
    That we one jot of former love retain.
Now at the last gasp of Love's latest breath,
    When, his pulse failing, Passion speechless lies,
When Faith is kneeling by his bed of death,
    And Innocence is closing up his eyes,
        Now if thou wouldst, when all have given him over,
        From death to life thou mightst him yet recover.

MICHAEL DRAYTON (1563–1631)

To His Coy Love: A Canzonet

I pray thee leave, love me no more,
Call home the Heart you gave me,
I but in vaine that Saint adore,
That can, but will not save me:

These poore halfe kisses kill me quite;
Was ever man thus served?
Amidst an Ocean of Delight,
For Pleasure to be sterved.

Shew me no more those Snowie Brests
With Azure Riverets branched,
Where whilst mine Eye with Plentie feasts,
Yet is my Thirst not stanched.
O Tantalus, thy Paines ne'er tell,
By me thou are prevented;
'Tis nothing to be plagu'd in Hell,
But thus in Heaven tormented.

Clip me no more in those deare Armes,
Nor thy Life's Comfort call me;
O, these are but too pow'rfull Charmes,
And doe but more inthrall me.
But see how patient I am growne,
In all this coyle about thee;
Come nice Thing, let thy Heart alone,
I cannot live without thee.

WILLIAM SHAKESPEARE (1564–1616)

Feste's Song from Twelfth Night

O mistress mine, where are you roaming?
O! stay and hear; your true love's coming,
    That can sing both high and low.
Trip no further, pretty sweeting;
Journeys end in lovers meeting,
    Every wise man's son doth know.

What is love? 'Tis not hereafter;
Present mirth hath present laughter;
    What's to come is still unsure.
In delay there lies no plenty;
Then come kiss me, sweet and twenty;
    Youth's a stuff will not endure.

WILLIAM SHAKESPEARE (1564–1616)

At the Moated Grange

Take, O! take those lips away,
   That so sweetly were forsworn,
And those eyes, the break of day,
   Lights that do mislead the morn;
But my kisses bring again,
     Bring again,
Seals of love, but sealed in vain,
     Sealed in vain.

BEN JONSON (1573–1637)

To Celia

Drink to me only with thine eyes,
　　And I will pledge with mine;
Or leave a kiss but in the cup
　　And I'll not look for wine.
The thirst that from the soul doth rise
　　Doth ask a drink divine;
But might I of Jove's nectar sup,
　　I would not change for thine.

I sent thee late a rosy wreath,
　　Not so much honouring thee
As giving it a hope that there
　　It could not withered be;
But thou thereon didst only breathe,
　　And sent'st it back to me;
Since when it grows, and smells, I swear,
　　Not of itself but thee!

ANONYMOUS (18TH CENTURY)

I gently touched her hand: she gave
A look that did my soul enslave;
I pressed her rebel lips in vain:
They rose up to be pressed again.
   Thus happy, I no farther meant,
   Than to be pleased and innocent.

On her soft breasts my hand I laid,
And a quick, light impression made;
They with a kindly warmth did glow,
And swelled, and seemed to overflow.
   Yet, trust me, I no farther meant,
   Than to be pleased and innocent.

On her eyes my eyes did stay:
O'er her smooth limbs my hands did stray;
Each sense was ravished with delight,
And my soul stood prepared for flight.
   Blame me not if at last I meant
   More to be pleased than innocent.

"The Stolen Kiss" by Jean Honoré Fragonard, circa 1761–1765.

JAMES LEIGH HUNT (1784–1859)

Jenny Kissed Me

Jenny kissed me when we met,
　Jumping from the chair she sat in;
Time, you thief, who love to get
　Sweets into your list, put that in!
Say I'm weary, say I'm sad,
　Say that health and wealth have missed me,
Say I'm growing old, but add,
　Jenny kissed me.

GEORGE GORDON NOEL, LORD BYRON (1788–1824)

When We Two Parted

When we two parted
  In silence and tears,
Half broken-hearted
  To sever for years,
Pale grew thy cheek and cold,
  Colder thy kiss;
Truly that hour foretold
  Sorrow to this.

The dew of the morning
  Sunk chill on my brow—
It felt like the warning
  Of what I feel now.
Thy vows are all broken,
  And light is thy fame;
I hear thy name spoken,
  And share in its shame.

They name thee before me,
  A knell to mine ear;
A shudder comes o'er me—
  Why wert thou so dear?
They know not I knew thee,
  Who knew thee too well:—
Long, long shall I rue thee,
  Too deeply to tell.

In secret we met—
  In silence I grieve,
That thy heart could forget,
  Thy spirit deceive.
If I should meet thee
  After long years,
How should I greet thee?
  With silence and tears.

PERCY BYSSHE SHELLEY (1792–1822)

Love's Philosophy

The fountains mingle with the river
    And the rivers with the Ocean,
The winds of Heaven mix for ever
    With a sweet emotion;
Nothing in the world is single;
    All things by a law divine
In one spirit meet and mingle.
    Why not I with thine?—

See the mountains kiss high Heaven
    And the waves clasp one another;
No sister-flower would be forgiven
    If it disdained its brother;
And the sunlight clasps the earth
    And the moonbeams kiss the sea:
What is all this sweet work worth
    If thou kiss not me?

JOHN KEATS (1795–1821)

I cry your mercy—pity—love!—aye, love!
    Merciful love that tantalizes not,
One-thoughted, never-wandering, guileless love,
    Unmasked, and being seen—without a blot!
O! let me have thee whole,—all—all—be mine!
    That shape, that fairness, that sweet minor zest
Of love, your kiss,—those hands, those eyes divine,
    That warm, white, lucent, million-pleasured breast,
Yourself—your soul—in pity give me all,
    Withhold no atom's atom or I die,
Or living on perhaps, your wretched thrall,
    Forget, in the mist of idle misery,
Life's purposes,—the palate of my mind
Losing its gust, and my ambition blind!

JOHN KEATS (1795–1821)

La Belle Dame Sans Merci

'O what can ail thee, knight-at-arms,
  Alone and palely loitering?
The sedge has withered from the lake,
  And no birds sing.

'O what can ail thee, knight-at-arms,
  So haggard and so woe-begone?
The squirrel's granary is full,
  And the harvest's done.

'I see a lily on thy brow
  With anguish moist and fever dew;
And on thy cheek a fading rose
  Fast withereth too.'

'I met a lady in the meads,
  Full beautiful—a faery's child,
Her hair was long, her foot was light,
  And her eyes were wild.

'I made a garland for her head,
  And bracelets too, and fragrant zone;
She looked at me as she did love,
  And made sweet moan.

'I set her on my pacing steed
  And nothing else saw all day long,
For sideways would she lean, and sing
  A faery's song.

'She found me roots of relish sweet,
  And honey wild and manna dew,
And sure in language strange she said,
  "I love thee true!"

'She took me to her elfin grot,
    And there she wept and sighed full sore;
And there I shut her wild, wild eyes
    With kisses four.

'And there she lulled me asleep,
    And there I dreamed—Ah! woe betide!
The latest dream I ever dreamed
    On the cold hill's side.

'I saw pale kings and princes too,
    Pale warriors, death-pale were they all;
Who cried—"La belle Dame sans Merci
    Hath thee in thrall!"

'I saw their starved lips in the gloam
    With horrid warning gaped wide,
And I awoke and found me here
    On the cold hill's side.

'And this is why I sojourn here
    Alone and palely loitering,
Though the sedge is withered from the lake,
    And no birds sing.'

THOMAS HOOD (1799–1845)

Ruth

She stood breast high amid the corn,
Clasped by the golden light of morn,
Like the sweetheart of the sun,
Who many a glowing kiss had won.

On her cheek an autumn flush,
Deeply ripened;—such a blush
In the midst of brown was born,
Like red poppies grown with corn.

Round her eyes her tresses fell,
Which were blackest none could tell,
But long lashes veiled a light,
that had else been all too bright.

And her hat, with shady brim,
Made her tressy forehead dim;—
Thus she stood amid the stooks,
Praising God with sweetest looks:—

Sure, I said, heaven did not mean,
Where I reap thou shouldst but glean,
Lay thy sheaf adown and come.
Share my harvest and my home.

FANNY KEMBLE (1809–1893)

Sonnet

Lady, whom my beloved loves so well!
When on his clasping arm thy head reclineth,
When on thy lips his ardent kisses dwell,
And the bright flood of burning light that shineth
In his dark eyes, is poured into thine;
When thou shalt lie enfolded to his heart
In all the trusting helplessness of love;
If in such joy sorrow can find a part,
Oh, give one sigh unto a doom like mine!
Which I would have thee pity, but not prove.
One cold, calm, careless, wintry look that fell
Haply by chance on one, is all that he
Ever gave my love; round that, my wild thoughts dwell
In one eternal pang of memory.

ROBERT BROWNING (1812–1889)

from In a Gondola

The moth's kiss, first!
Kiss me as if you made believe
You were not sure, this eve,
How my face, your flower, had pursed
Its petals up; so, here and there
You brush it, till I grow aware
Who wants me, and wide ope I burst.

The bee's kiss, now!
Kiss me as if you entered gay
My heart at some noonday,
A bud that dares not disallow
The claim, so all is rendered up,
And passively its shattered cup
Over your head to sleep I bow.

MATTHEW ARNOLD (1822–1888)

Longing

Come to me in my dreams, and then
By day I shall be well again!
For then the night will more than pay
The hopeless longing of the day.

Come, as thou cam'st a thousand times,
A messenger from radiant climes,
And smile on thy new world, and be
As kind to others as to me!

Or, as thou never cam'st in sooth,
Come now, and let me dream it truth;
And part my hair, and kiss my brow,
And say: *My love! why sufferest thou?*

Come to me in my dreams, and then
By day I shall be well again!
For then the night will more than pay
The hopeless longing of the day.

COVENTRY PATMORE (1823–1896)

The Kiss

'I saw you take his kiss!' ''Tis true.'
  'O, modesty!' ''Twas strictly kept:
He thought me asleep; at least I knew
    He thought I thought he thought I slept.'

ALGERNON CHARLES SWINBURNE (1837–1909)

In the Orchard

Leave go my hands, let me catch breath and see;
Let the dew-fall drench either side of me;
   Clear apple-leaves are soft upon that moon
Seen sidelong like a blossom in the tree;
   And God, ah God, that day should be so soon.

The grass is thick and cool, it lets us lie.
Kissed upon either cheek and either eye,
   I turn to thee as some green afternoon
Turns toward sunset, and is loth to die;
   Ah God, ah God, that day should be so soon.

Lie closer, lean your face upon my side,
Feel where the dew fell that has hardly dried,
   Hear how the blood beats that went nigh to swoon;
The pleasure lives there when the sense had died,
   Ah God, ah God, that day should be so soon.

O my fair lord, I charge you leave me this:
Is it not sweeter than a foolish kiss?
   Nay take it then, my flower, my first in June,
My rose, so like a tender mouth it is:
   Ah God, ah God, that day should be so soon.

Love, till dawn sunder night from day with fire
Dividing my delight and my desire,
   The crescent life and love the plenilune,
Love me though dusk begin and dark retire;
   Ah God, ah God, that day should be so soon.

Ah, my heart fails, my blood draws back; I know,
When life runs over, life is near to go;
    And with the slain of love love's ways are strewn,
And with their blood, if love will have it so;
    Ah God, ah God, that day should be so soon.

Ah, do thy will now; slay me if thou wilt;
There is no building now the walls are built,
    No quarrying now the corner-stone is hewn,
No drinking now the vine's whole blood is spilt;
    Ah God, ah God, that day should be so soon.

Nay, slay me now; nay, for I will be slain;
Pluck thy red pleasure from the teeth of pain,
    Break down thy vine ere yet grape-gatherers prune,
Slay me ere day can slay desire again;
    Ah God, ah God, that day should be so soon.

Yea, with thy sweet lips, with thy sweet sword; yea
Take life and all, for I will die, I say;
    Love, I gave love, is life a better boon?
For sweet night's sake I will not live till day;
    Ah God, ah God, that day should be so soon.

Nay, I will sleep then only; nay, but go.
Ah sweet, too sweet to me, my sweet, I know
    Love, sleep, and death go to the sweet same tune;
Hold my hair fast, and kiss me through it soon.
    Ah God, ah God, that day should be so soon.

ALGERNON CHARLES SWINBURNE (1837–1909)

Kissing Her Hair

Kissing her hair I sat against her feet,
Wove and unwove it, wound and found it sweet;
Made fast therewith her hands, drew down her eyes,
Deep as deep flowers and dreamy like dim skies;
With her own tresses bound and found her fair,
Kissing her hair.

Sleep were no sweeter than her face to me,
Sleep of cold sea-bloom under the cold sea;
What pain could get between my face and hers?
What new sweet thing would love not relish worse?
Unless, perhaps, white death had kissed me there,
Kissing her hair?

THOMAS HARDY (1840–1928)

Two Lips

I kissed them in fancy as I came
　　Away in the morning glow:
I kissed them through the glass of her picture-frame:
　　She did not know.

I kissed them in love, in troth, in laughter,
　　When she knew all; long so!
That I should kiss them in a shroud thereafter
　　She did not know.

THOMAS HARDY (1840–1928)

On the Departure Platform

We kissed at the barrier; and passing through
She left me, and moment by moment got
Smaller and smaller, until to my view
   She was but a spot;

A wee white spot of muslin fluff
That down the diminishing platform bore
Through hustling crowds of gentle and rough
   To the carriage door.

Under the lamplight's fitful glowers,
Behind dark groups from far and near,
Whose interests were apart from ours,
   She would disappear,

Then show again, till I ceased to see
That flexible form, that nebulous white;
And she who was more than my life to me
   Had vanished quite.

We have penned new plans since that fair fond day,
And in season she will appear again—
Perhaps in the same soft white array—
   But never as then!

—'And why, young man, must eternally fly
A joy you'll repeat, if you love her well?'
—O friend, nought happens twice thus; why,
   I cannot tell!

ERNEST DOWSON (1867–1910)

Non Sum Qualis Eram Bonae Sub Regno Cynarae

Last night, ah, yesternight, betwixt her lips and mine
There fell thy shadow, Cynara! thy breath was shed
Upon my soul between the kisses and the wine;
And I was desolate and sick of an old passion,
Yea, I was desolate and bowed my head:
I have been faithful to thee, Cynara! in my fashion.

All night upon mine heart I felt her warm heart beat,
Night-long within mine arms in love and sleep she lay;
Surely the kisses of her bought red mouth were sweet;
But I was desolate and sick of an old passion,
When I awoke and found the dawn was gray:
I have been faithful to thee, Cynara! in my fashion.

I have forgot much, Cynara! gone with the wind,
Flung roses, roses riotously with the throng,
Dancing, to put thy pale, lost lilies out of mind;
But I was desolate and sick of an old passion,
Yea, all the time, because the dance was long:
I have been faithful to thee, Cynara! in my fashion.

I cried for madder music and for stronger wine,
But when the feast is finished and the lamps expire,
Then falls thy shadow, Cynara! the night is thine;
And I am desolate and sick of an old passion,
Yea hungry for the lips of my desire:
I have been faithful to thee, Cynara! in my fashion.

ALFRED NOYES (1880–1958)

The Highwayman

Part One

The wind was a torrent of darkness among the gusty trees,
The moon was a ghostly galleon tossed upon cloudy seas,
The road was a ribbon of moonlight over the purple moor,
      And the highwayman came riding,
      Riding, riding,
The highwayman came riding, up to the old inn-door.

He'd a French cocked-hat on his forehead, a bunch of lace at
    his chin,
A coat of the claret velvet, and breeches of brown doe-skin;
They fitted with never a wrinkle: his boots were up to the thigh!
      And he rode with a jeweled twinkle,
      His pistol butts a-twinkle,
His rapier hilt a-twinkle, under the jeweled sky.

Over the cobbles he clattered and clashed in the dark inn-yard,
And he tapped with his whip on the shutters, but all was locked
    and barred;
He whistled a tune to the window, and who should be waiting
    there
      But the landlord's black-eyed daughter,
      Bess, the landlord's daughter,
Plaiting a dark red love-knot into her long black hair.

And dark in the dark old inn-yard a stable-wicket creaked
Where Tim the ostler listened; his face was white and peaked;
His eyes were hollows of madness, his hair like mouldy hay,
      But he loved the landlord's daughter,
      The landlord's red-lipped daughter,
Dumb as a dog he listened, and he heard the robber say:

"One kiss, my bonny sweetheart, I'm after a prize tonight,
But I shall be back with the yellow gold before the morning light;
Yet, if they press me sharply, and harry me through the day,
             Then look for me by moonlight,
             Watch for me by moonlight,
I'll come to thee by moonlight, though hell should bar the way."

He rose upright in the stirrups; he scarce could reach her hand,
But she loosened her hair i' the casement! His face burnt like
        a brand
As the black cascade of perfume came tumbling over his breast;
             And he kissed its waves in the moonlight,
             (Oh, sweet black waves in the moonlight!)
Then he tugged at his rein in the moonlight, and galloped away
        to the West.

MAY PROBYN (1881–1895)

Barcarolle

Last night we sailed, my love and I,
Last night and years ago—
Was it moon or sea, we drifted through?
I think I shall never know!
We had no oar—
We neared no shore—
We floated with the tide;
The moon was white,
And the sea alight,
And none in the world beside.

I and my love, we said farewell—
It is years and years away.
We kissed our last in a life gone by—
I think it was yesterday!
Oh! for heaven, give me
A moon and a sea
To sail, when we both have died,
With never an oar—
With never a shore—
Drifting on with the tide!

Finnish Poems

"The Kiss" by Edvard Munch, 1902.

J.L. RUNEBERG (1804–1877)

Three teachings the mother gave her daughter:
Not to sigh, not to be unhappy,
and never to kiss a boy—

Mother, if your daughter does submit,
does submit to your last advice
she shall surely disobey the first two.

translated by Börje Vähämäki

"Spring passes quickly,
more quickly yet summer,
fall dwells much longer.
O lovely cheeks, away
you soon will wither,
and never bud again."

The boy to that responded:
"Still in the days of autumn
spring's memories delight us,
still in the days of winter
summer's harvests provide us.
Freely spring may pass away,
freely too the cheeks may wither,
Let us now but love each other,
let us now be kissing!"

translated by Börje Vähämäki

J.L. RUNEBERG (1804–1877)

The First Kiss

On the edge of a silverlined cloud sat the Evening Star,
from the dusk of the valley the maiden queried:
"Tell me, Evening Star, what thoughts are harboured in heaven,
when the first kiss is planted on a lover's lips?"

Heaven's bashful daughter was heard saying:
"Down on earth the angels of light keep glancing
their own bliss they see reflected;
only death casts down his eyes—and weeps."

translated by Börje Vähämäki

Missing Him

Should my treasure come
my darling step by
I'd know him by his coming
recognize him by his step
though he were still a mile off
or two miles away.
As mist I'd go out
as smoke I would reach the yard
as sparks I would speed
as flame I would fly;
I'd bowl along beside him
pout before his face.

I would touch his hand
though a snake were in his palm
I would kiss his mouth
though doom stared him in the face
I'd climb on his neck
though death were on his neck bones
I'd stretch beside him
though his side were all bloody.
And yet my treasure has not
his mouth bloody from a wolf
his hands greasy from a snake
nor his neck in death's clutches:
his mouth is of melted fat
his lips are as of honey
his hands golden, fair
his neck like a heather stalk.

translated by Keith Bosley

FROM THE KANTELETAR (1840)

Good Night — Farewell

To my love, I say: "Good evening."
Little bird, I say: "Good evening."
Like a little bird is my darling, is my darling.
Dancing, dancing, with my darling,
swirling, whirling with my dearest,
Dancing, swirling, whirling
together with my loved one!
Stand here with me, O my dearest,
stand here with me, O my darling,
stand beside me now,
O my loved one, stand beside me!
Your hand, give to me, my dearest,
your hand, give to me, my darling,
your hand, give to me,
O my loved one, O my loved one!
Come, embrace me now, my dearest,
Come, embrace me now, my sweetheart,
Come, embrace me now, my loved one.
Lost in fond embrace
are we now, my own, my darling!
Kiss me, kiss me, kiss me, dearest,
kiss me, kiss me, kiss me, sweetheart.
O embrace me now, my dearest.
O embrace me now,
Come to me, my own, my darling!
Kiss me, kiss me,
kiss me, O my darling, kiss me!
O my darling, kiss me!
Farewell now, my own, my dearest,
Farewell now, my own, my sweetheart,
Farewell now, my own, my darling,
Now farewell, my darling,
my dearest, my most beloved one!

translated by Norman Luboff

KATRI VALA (1901–1944)

The memories of all the passionate embraces
are lost behind the days.

But once
you quietly kissed my forehead
as you left me
in the gentle snowfall.
And all around was white tenderness
So lovely, so tearful.

The memory of that moment
unfolds during blue nights
like a quiet flower
replete with fragile fragrance,
and my heart is filled
only with trembling goodness.

translated by Börje Vähämäki

YRJÖ JYLHÄ (1903–1956)

Shadows

As the moon shines
I am jealous of my own shadow.
As my shadow melts together with your
    shadow on the snow
I watch it dejectedly.

I may kiss your thirsty lips
and your burning skin,
your splended, fragrant body
I may conquer hundredfold—

yet for me that is not enough!
I want to tear you open,
I want to merge with you
as our two shadows merge.

translated by Börje Vähämäki

French Poems

Illustration by Maurice Leloir.

MARIE DE FRANCE (13ᵀᴴ CENTURY)

Song from Chaitivel

Hath any loved you well, down there,
Summer or winter through?
Down there, have you found any fair
Laid in the grave with you?
Is death's long kiss a richer kiss
Than mine was wont to be—
Or have you gone to some far bliss
And quite forgotten me?

What soft enamouring of sleep
Hath you in some soft way?
What charmed death holdeth you with deep
Strange lure by night and day?
A little space below the grass,
Out of the sun and shade;
But worlds away from me, alas,
Down there where you are laid.
My bright is vaved and wasted gold,
What is it now to thee—
Whether the rose-red life I hold
Or white death holdeth me?
Down there you love the grave's own green,
And evermore you rave
Of some sweet seraph you have seen
Or dreamt of in the grave.

There you shall lie as you have lain,
Though in the world above,
Another live your life again,
Loving again your love:
Is it not sweet beneath the palm?
Is it not warm day rife
With some long mystic golden calm
Better than love and life?

The broad quaint odorous leaves like hands
Weaving the fair day through,
Weave sleep no burnished bird withstands,
While death weaves sleep for you;
And many a strange rich breathing sound
Ravishes morn and noon:
And in that place you must have found
Death a delicious swoon—

Hold me no longer for a word
I used to say or sing:
Ah, long ago you must have heard
So many a sweeter thing:
For rich earth must have reached your heart
And turned the faith to flowers;
And warm wind stolen, part by part,
Your soul through faithless hours.
And many a soft seed must have won
Soil of some yielding thought,
To bring a bloom up to the sun
That else had ne'er been brought;
And, doubtless, many a passionate hue
Hath made that place more fair,
Making some passionate part of you
Faithless to me down there.

translated by A. O'Shaughnessy

CHARLES OF ORLEANS (1391–1465)

My ghostly father, I me confess,
   First to God and then to you,
   That at a window—wot ye how?—
I stole a kiss of great sweetness,
Which done was out avisedness;
   But it is done not undone now.
My ghostly father, I me confess,
   First to God and then to you.
But I restore it shall doubtless
   Again, if so be that I mow;
   And that to God I make a vow
And else I ask forgiveness.
My ghostly father, I me confess,
   First to God and then to you.

---

ghostly father spiritual father, priest
out avisedness without thought

CLÉMENT MAROT (1495–1544)

A Love-Lesson

A sweet "No! no!" with a sweet smile beneath
Becomes an honest girl, I'd have you learn it;
As for plain, "Yes!" it may be said, i' faith,
Too plainly and too soft, pray, well discern it!

Not that I'd have my pleasure incomplete,
Or lose the kiss for which my lips beset you;
But that in suffering me to take it, sweet!
I'd have you say: "No! no! I will not let you!"

translated by Leigh Hunt

PIERRE DE RONSARD (1524–1585)

Deadly Kisses

Ah, take these lips away; no more,
No more such kisses give to me.
My spirit faints for joy; I see
Through mists of death the dreamy shore,
And meadows by the water-side,
Where all about the Hollow Land
Fare the sweet singers that have died,
With their lost ladies, hand in hand;
Ah, Love, bow fireless are their eyes,
How pale their lips that kiss and smile.
So mine must be in little while
If thou wilt kiss me in such wise.

translated by Andrew Lang

Illustration by Maurice Leloir.

PIERRE DE RONSARD (1524–1585)

To His Mistress

Many of their freed bodies
Discovered themselves in strange countries
Changed in miraculous ways,
One to a serpent, another to a stone.

One into a flower, another into a shrub,
One into a wolf, another into a dove,
One was changed into a stream,
And one into a swallow.

I would be a mirror.
You would always look into me.
I could be your shirt.
You would wear me.

With great delight I would become
Water while I bathed your body;
And become the perfume of you,
And give you my scent.

I would be the ribbon binding
Your lovely breasts.
I would be the necklace
Around your lovely throat.

I want to be the coral
That your lips are touching.
All night and day I would kiss
Your sweet lips and mouth.

LOUISE LABÉ (1526–1566)

Povre Âme Amoureuse

(Sapphics)

When to my lone soft bed at eve returning
Sweet desir'd sleep already stealeth o'er me,
My spirit flieth to the fairy-land of her tyrannous love.
Him then I think fondly to kiss, to hold him
Frankly then to my bosom; I that all day
Have looked for him suffering, repining, yea many long days.
O bless'd sleep, with flatteries beguile me;
So, if I ne'er may of a surety have him,
Grant to my poor soul amorous the dark gift of this illusion.

translated by Robert Bridges

JACQUES TAHUREAU (1527–1555)

Moonlight

The high Midnight was garlanding her head
With many a shining star in shining skies,
And, of her grace, a slumber on mine eyes,
And, after sorrow, quietness was shed.
Far in dim fields cicadas jargoned
A thin shrill clamor of complaints and cries;
And all the woods were pallid, in strange wise,
With pallor of the sad moon overspread.

Then came my lady to that lonely place,
And, from her palfrey stooping, did embrace
And hang upon my neck, and kissed me over;
Wherefore the day is far less dear than night,
And sweeter is the shadow than the light,
Since night has made me such a happy lover.

translated by Andrew Lang

JACQUES TAHUREAU (1527–1555)

Shadows of His Lady

Within the sand of what far river lies
The gold that gleams in tresses of my Love?
What highest circle of the Heavens above
Is jeweled with such stars as are her eyes?
And where is the rich sea whose coral vies
With her red lips, that cannot kiss enough?
What dawn-lit garden knew the rose, whereof
The fled soul lives in her cheeks' rosy guise?

What Parian marble that is loveliest,
Can make the whiteness of her brow and breast?
When drew she breath from the Sabæn glade?
Oh, happy rock and river, sky and sea,
Gardens and glades Sabæn, all that be
The far-off splendid semblance of my maid.

Illustration by Maurice Leloir.   *translated by Andrew Lang*

THÉOPHILE DE VIAU (1591–1626)

Sleep

I've kissed thee, sweetheart, in a dream at least,
And though the core of love is in me still,
This joy, that in my sense did softly thrill,
The ardor of my longing hath appeased
And by this tender strife my spirit, eased,
And half consoled, I soothe myself, until
I find my heart from all its pain released.
My senses, hushed, begin to fall on sleep,
Slumber, for which two weary nights I weep,
Takes thy dear place at last within my eyes,
And though so cold he is, as all men vow,
For me he breaks his natural icy guise,
And shows himself more warm and fond than thou.

translated by Edmund Gosse

VICTOR HUGO (1802–1885)

To a Woman

Child! if I were a king, my throne I would surrender,
My scepter, and my car, and kneeling vavassours,
My golden crown, and porphyry baths, and consorts tender,
And fleets that fill the seas, and regal pomp and splendor,
    All for one look of yours!

If I were God, the earth and luminous deeps that span it,
Angels and demons bowed beneath my word divine,
Chaos profound, with flanks of flaming gold and granite,
Eternity, and space, and sky, and sun, and planet,
    All for one kiss of thine.

translated by W. J. Robertson

THÉOPHILE GAUTIER (1811–1872)

Posthumous Coquetry

Let there be laid, when I am dead,
Ere 'neath the coffin-lid I lie,
Upon my cheek a little red,
A little black about the eye.

For I in my close bier would fain,
As on the night his vows were made,
Rose-red eternally remain,
With kohl beneath my blue eye laid.

Wind me no shroud of linen down
My body to my feet, but fold
The white folds of my muslin gown
With thirteen flounces as of old.

This shall go with me where I go:
I wore it when I won his heart;
His first look hallowed it, and so,
For him, I laid the gown apart.

No immortelles, no broidered grace
Of tears upon my cushions be;
Lay me on my pillow's lace,
My hair across it like a sea.

That pillow, those mad nights of old,
Has seen our slumbering brows unite,
And 'neath the gondola's black fold
Has counted kisses infinite.

Between my hands of ivory,
Together set for prayer and rest,
Place then the opal rosary
The holy Pope at Rome has blest

I will lie down then on that bed
And sleep the sleep that shall not cease;
His mouth upon my mouth has said
Pater and *Ave* for my peace.

translated by Arthur Symons

"Qui Trop Embrasse" by Tito, circa 1920.

THÉOPHILE GAUTIER (1811–1872)

To A Pink Dress

How I like you in that dress
which undresses you so well,
making your round breasts firm,
showing your naked white arm.

As delicate as a bee's wing,
cool as the heart of tea-rose,
it hovers around your beauty
like a beautiful, rosy caress.

Silver shivers of silk glide on
your skin and the cloth sends
back its reflected image to
the pink lights of your flesh.

Where did you find such a dress,
one that seems to be made from
your flesh, a living cloth which
mingles its pink with your skin?

Are these secret hues taken
from the crimson of the dawn,
from the shell of Venus, or from
your nipples about to burst forth?

Or is the cloth dyed in the roses
of your modesty? No, but after
being painted more than twenty times,
your body knows its own splendor.

Throwing off this oppressive veil,
you would be the reality which art
dreams of, like Princess Borghese,
you would pose for Canova.

And these pink folds are the lips
of my unsatisfied desire, which you torment,
dressing your body
with a tunic of kisses.

PAUL VERLAINE (1844–1896)

Lettre
From *Fêtes galantes*

Far from your side removed by thankless cares
(The gods are witness when a lover swears)
I languish and I die, Madame, as still
My use is, which I punctually fulfill,
And go, through heavy-hearted woes conveyed,
Attended ever by your lovely shade,
By day in thought, by night in dreams of hell,
So that at length my dwindling body lost
In very soul, I too become a ghost,
I too, and in the lamentable stress
Of vain desires remembering happiness,
Remembered kisses, now, alas, unfelt,
My shadow shall into your shadow melt.

Meanwhile, dearest, your most obedient slave.

How does the sweet society behave,
Thy cat, thy dog, thy parrot? and is she
Still, as of old, the black-eyed Silvanie
(I had loved black eyes if thine had not been blue)
Who ogled me at moments, palsambleu!
Thy tender friend and thy sweet confidant?
One dream there is, Madame, long wont to haunt
This too impatient heart: to put the earth
And all its treasures (of how little worth!)

Before your feet as tokens of a love
Equal to the most famous flames that move
The hearts of men to conquer all but death.
Cleopatra was less loved, yes, on my faith,
By Antony or Caesar than you are,
Madame, by me, who truly would by far
Out-do the deeds of Caesar for a smile,
O Cleopatra, Queen of word and wile,
Or, for a kiss, take flight with Antony.

With this, farewell, dear, and no more from me;
How can the time it takes to read it, quite
Be worth the trouble that it took to write?

translated by Arthur Symons

GUY DE MAUPASSANT (1850–1893)

Desires

The dream of one is to have wings and follow
The soaring heights of space with clamorous cries;
With lissome fingers seize the supple swallow
And lose himself in somber gulfs of skies.

Another would have strength with circling shoulder
To crush the wrestler in his close embrace;
And, not with yielding loins or blood grown colder,
Stop, with one stroke, wild steeds in frantic chase.

What I love best is loveliness corporeal:
I would be beautiful as gods of old;
So from my radiant limbs love immemorial
In hearts of men a living flame should hold.

I would have women love me in wild fashion—
Choose one today and with tomorrow change;
Pleased, when I pass, to pluck the flower of passion,
As fruits are plucked when forth the fingers range.

Each leaves upon the lips a different flavor;
These diverse savors bid their sweetness grow.
My fond caress would fly with wandering favor
From dusky locks to locks of golden glow.

But most of all I love the unlooked-for meeting,
Those ardors in the blood loosed by a glance,
The conquests of an hour, as swiftly fleeting,
Kisses exchanged at the sole will of chance.

At daybreak I would dote on the dark charmer,
Whose clasping arms cling close in amorous swoon;
And, lulled at eve by the blonde siren's murmur,
Gaze on her pale brow silvered by the moon.

Then my calm heart, that holds no haunting specter,
Would lightly towards a fresh chimera haste:
Enough in these delights to sip the nectar,
For in the dregs there lurks a bitter taste.

translated by W. J. Robertson

ALBERT SAMAIN (1858–1900)

Sleepless Night

Tonight there shall be lighted here no tapers,
But a sheaf of still wet flowers that shake
    in frailness
Shall light thy chamber—where thy tender
    paleness
Shall like a dream be drowned in white
    gauze vapors.

That we may breathe a bliss without alloy,
On the sad piano where the flowers shake
Play thou a song of angels' hearts that ache,
And I shall swoon into a trancèd joy.

So we will love, mute and austere. Save this,
That sometimes on thy slender hand a kiss
Shall be the drop that overflows the urn.

Sister! And in the skies that o'er us bend
The chaste desire of passion taciturn
Shall slowly like a silver star ascend.

translated by Jethro Bithell

Illustration by Maurice Leloir.

FRANCIS VIELÉ-GRIFFIN (1864–1937)

Now the Sweet Eves are Withered

Now the sweet eves are withered like the flowers of October
—What should we tell the willow, and the reeds, and the
   lagoons!
My soul forever has grown gray and sober;
—What should we tell the dunes?

The wind arising comes without a word discreetly:
Fresh with your kisses is my brow;
The night—as mothers comfort sweetly—
Comes with a cradling kiss to greet me,
What should we tell the willow now?

While the spring bloomed you were my King, my Poet,
You with your sweet words were the King of Hearts;
But while we two were laughing, did we know it,
That both of us were playing ancient parts?

O you and I, did either of us know it?
—Now all is gray where we would go—
We with our false and honeyed laughter?
What knew we of the dark times coming after?
What did we know?

There were old poems, doubtless, singing to me;
To you, old tales of fortune crowning doles;
"You love me then?—I love you!—Love me truly!"

Were we so young to laugh at our own souls!
What should we go and say now to the dunes?
What to the willow, to the reeds, lagoons?
—The moon is rising in pale aureoles—
Our hearts forgave, and died like misty moons.

translated by Jethro Bithell

ANDRÉ SPIRE (1868–1966)

Spring

Now hand in hand, you little maidens, walk.
Pass in the shadow of the crumbling wall.
Arch your proud bellies under rosy aprons.
And let your eyes so deeply lucid tell
Your joy at feeling flowing into your heart
Another loving heart that blends with yours;
You children faint with being hand in hand.
Walk hand in hand, you languorous maidens, walk.
The boys are turning round, and drinking in
Your sensual petticoats that beat your heels.
And, while you swing your interlacing hands,
Tell, with your warm mouths yearning each to each,
The first books you have read, and your first kisses.
Walk hand in hand, you maidens, friend with friend.

Walk hand in hand, you lovers loving silence.
Walk to the sun that veils itself with willows.
Trail your uneasy limbs by languorous banks,
The stream is full of dusk, your souls are heavy.
You silent lovers, wander hand in hand.

translated by Jethro Bithell

"Daphnis and Chloé"
by Pierre Bonnard, 1902

ROBERT DESNOS (1900–1945)

To a Mysterious Woman

I have dreamed so much of you that you have become unreal.

Is there still time to reach that living body and to kiss
on those lips the birth of the voice that is so dear to me?

I have dreamed so much of you that my arms, accustomed to
being crossed on my chest while embracing your shadow,
    would not
bend to enfold your body.

And that, faced with the reality of what has haunted me and
ruled me for days and years, I should doubtless become a
    shadow myself.

O emotional fulcrum.

I have dreamed so much of you that there is no time for me
to awaken. I am half asleep while I stand, my body exposed to
    all the
appearances of life and love and you, who alone count for me
    today,
I could no more touch your brow and your lips than the brow
    and
the lips of any woman I met.

I have dreamed so much of you, so often walked, talked,
slept with your phantom that perhaps the only thing still left
    for me
is to be a ghost among ghosts and a hundred times more than a
ghost who walks and will move joyfully on the sundial of your life.

German Poems

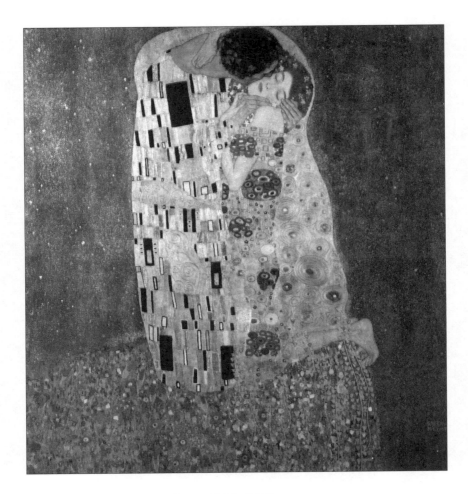

"The Kiss" by Gustav Klimt, 1907–1908.

FRANZ GRILLPARZER (1791–1872)

A Kiss

A hand is to be kissed with reverence,
The forehead—solemnly, with friendship,
The cheeks—with tender admiration,
And the lips be kissed with ardor,
While the eyes one kisses with langour,
The neck—with passionate desire,
And with a maddening delirium
All the rest is to be kissed.

translated by Ann Zeller

OTTO JULIUS BIERBAUM (1865–1910)

Come Here and Let Me Kiss You

The air is as if full of violins,
From all the flourishing branches
A white wonder pours down;
Spring rages in the blood,
This is the best time
For all kinds of merriment.

Come here and let me kiss you!
You must submit
To my arm embracing you.
Knocking and shaking
Goes through the whole life:
That is the red blood, it sings, it sings.

translated by Ann Zeller

❧ Greek Poems ❧

"L'éternel Printemps" by Auguste Rodin, 1884.

PLATO (429–347 B.C.)

Sokrates to His Lover

As I kissed Agathon my soul swelled to my lips,
where it hangs, pitiful, hoping to leap across.

MELEAGROS (140–70 B.C.)

The Wine Cup

The wine cup is happy. It rubbed against
warm Zenophilia's erotic mouth. O bliss!
I wish she would press her lips under my lips
and in one breathless gulp drain down my soul.

The Kiss

Your eyes are fire, Timarian, your kiss birdlime.
You look at me and I burn. You touch me and I
stick!

NIKARCHOS (1ˢᵀ CENTURY A.D.)

Kissing

If you kiss me you hate me; if you hate me
you kiss me,
but if you don't hate me, my sweet friend,
don't kiss me.

Hungarian Poems

JÁNOS GARAY (1812–1853)

To My Bride

I embrace you,
Finally embrace you!
My burning love
Enchanting due!

Mine the pretty eyes;
To see bliss concealed,
To gaze into them,
Is heaven revealed.

Mine the little mouth,
Whose darling mistress,
In her kissing
Is loving sweetness;

Mine the beautiful
Snow-white breasts,
With noble, ardent
Feelings blessed.

Which from your eyes
Flame into mine;
And which your lips
Kiss into mine;

Whose beneficence
In your bosom is found,
Oh my lady, I'm
in your love bound.

And with this love
In paradise to be,
Is happiness eternal
Blooming for me.

Oh lady, this feeling
So sweet, so great!
No, it's not a dream!
You are my sweet mate!

translated by Katherine Gyékényesi Gatto

SÁNDOR PETÖFI (1823–1849)

How Shall I Call You?

How shall I call you,
When in the dreaming afterlight
I look in wonder on the evening star
Of your fair eyes,
As if discovering I looked
Upon this star
And every ray
A brook of love
To flow into the ocean of my soul . . .
How shall I call you?

How shall I call you,
When you let fly at me
Your glance,
This gentle dove,
Each feather of whose plumage is
An olive branch of tranquil peace,
Caressing to the touch and kind!
Softer far than silk
And gentle as the cradle's pillow . . .
How shall I call you?

How shall I call you,
When sounds the vibrant music of your voice,
And if the trees now winterbound
Could only hear those lovely notes,
Green leaves would deck their boughs
For they would then believe
That Spring is here!—
Deliverer and long awaited one—
Because they hear the lark . . .
How shall I call you?

How shall I call you,
When my lips brush
The burning rubies of your lips,
And in a kiss of fire our souls melt into one,
As dawn melts darkness into day—
When world is gone from me,
And time is gone,
When I am deluged by eternity with all
The mysteries of utter bliss . . .
How shall I call you?

How shall I call you,
The sweetest mother of delight,
The fairy daughter of a fantasy
That dared to storm the sky!—
My wildest dreams ashamed before
The blinding beauty of a truth!—
The only treasure of my soul,
The dearest treasure of the world,
So lovely, sweet and young
          . . . my wedded wife,
How shall I call you?

translated by Eugénie Bayard Pierce and Emil Delmár

LAJOS DÓCZI (1845–1919)

What is a Kiss?

Tis understood alone by those who lean
To listen, what a sweet, true kiss doth mean.
Therein there is no right, will, or intent;
Exchanging not, they mutually present—
Born of a minute, as though suddenly
Two sparks should catch and cause a flame to be.
Sweet is the kiss if sleep thy sweetheart sway;
What she might give thou tak'st in stealthy way;
But sweeter still if from the pouting lip
Denying and delaying thou dost sip.
But sweetest 'tis when both a thirst do feel,
And, giving, each from t'other fain would steal.
Yet, if desire exists where no claim lives,
It dares to take, but feels not that it gives;
Indeed, such kisses, which by hundreds thrive,
Not wedded yoke but sweet love keeps alive.
Even this is sweeter when earth's envious eyes,
Like falcon's, watch thee and thy honeyed prize.
The moment comes, thou feelest "now or never!"
Arms fly to arms, lips cling as though forever
Each would be first and each be last in bliss;
Each one is kissed and each doth warmly kiss.
Just as a diver to the depths doth leap,
So doth desire plunge in the moment's deep.
What rapture can a brief span not conceive?
If not forbidden, 'tis no kiss, believe!

translated by William N. Loew

ENDRE ADY (1877–1919)

A Half-Kissed Kiss

A half-kissed kiss is wildly before us
Blazing and flaming.
Cold is the evening. Sometimes we hasten,
Weeping we hasten,
Never attaining.

How often we stop. Together we mourn,
Freezing and burning.
Thou thrustest me back. Blood-stained are my lips,
Blood-stained are thy lips,
Yearning and yearning.

This kiss consumed we should peacefully
Die without sorrow.
We long for that kiss, we crave for that fire,
But sadly we say:
Tomorrow, tomorrow.

translated by R. Bonnerjea

LÖRINC SZABÓ (1900–1957)

Moments

Since yesterday when I kissed you
and you languishing (but just for a moment,
since you protested already) left
my knee between your trembling knees:
constantly gratitude renders you before me,
constantly you stand before me, on the street, at work
constantly I run into you: I see your head
bent back, your burning face,
your closed eyes and tortured beauteous desire's
beautiful smile on your lips.
At such a time I too close my eyes for just
a second and I feel faint:
I feel your nearness, my face bathes in the
sweet lines of your face, your burning breasts
scorch my hand, you kiss me again,
and I awaken terrified: oh, this is but
pure craziness—and still it feels so good
to lose myself in you: your entire body
flows around me and I happily
gallop away in your flaming veins.

translated by Katherine Gyékényesi Gatto

Indian Poems

"Vajrasattva in Union with the Supreme Wisdom Visvatara" Tibet,
Lamaistic-Tantric, 18ᵗʰ Century.

THE KAMASUTRA OF VATSYAYANA (1ˢᵗ CENTURY A.D.)

Kisses Classified

The passion-kindling kiss:
> When she looks at his face while he sleeps and kisses it to show her desire.

The distracted kiss:
> When she kisses him while he is inattentive or quarrelling or thinking of something else or sleepy.

The awakening kiss:
> When someone comes late at night and to show his desire kisses his beloved who is asleep on the bed.
> She may go on seeming to be asleep at the time of her lover's arrival in order to establish his inclinations.

The purposeful kiss:
> When someone kisses the reflection of the beloved in a mirror, in water or on a wall.

The transferred kiss:
> When someone kisses a child, a picture or a statue.

The challenging kiss:
> When a man comes up to a woman at night in the theatre or at a party and kisses her on the fingers, or on the toes if she is sitting.
> When a woman is massaging her lover and lays her head on his thigh as if overcome by sleep, and to arouse him kisses his thigh or his big toe.

And here there is a verse:
> Each act in kind should be repaid
> With stroke for stroke, and kiss for kiss

BIHARI LAL (HINDI)

Glimpses

Their glances stretched between the rooftops form
A tightrope for brave lovers' hearts to cross

First making sure none watches them, they stand on tiptoe
Then lean across the wall between for eager kisses

Up to the roof she goes to look, then down
Untiring, like a yo-yo on love's string

Above her yard she sees her lover's kite
And madly runs about to chase its shadow

You praise those pigeons tumbling in the sky
Who is it though who made you look so thrilled?

With arm around him, now she moves, then stops
Flashing like lightning on her balcony

Their hearts so full of love, their talk so full of pain
A million signals sent while walking to the door.

VEMANA (TELUGU)

Beginnings and endings

When he beholds the beauty of her form
And sees the wavings of her waist-long hair
Who can resist a lovely woman's charms?

Simply to see a lovely woman thrills
Us with a fever which can drive us mad—
Her teeth so flashed in a smile are something else!

Can men who stare at women know them as
They truly are? Desire destroys their sense
Dissolving them like gum that melts in flames.

A man who has feasted and sits at his ease
Has feelings of love at the sight of a woman
For food is the force which inflames his desire.

Both men and women when well-filled with food
Will say that Cupid is tormenting them
But empty stomachs make love powerless.

When love is past, those cherry lips taste like
The nightshade's berry of the poison-nut
Old passion's like the acid mango-leaf.

Irish Poems

Illustration by Peadar Mc Daid.

ANONYMOUS (9ᵀᴴ CENTURY)

He's a Sweetheart

He's a sweetheart
   a nut-filled grove,
Here's a kiss
   to the one I love.

translation by Gabriel Rosenstock

SEATHRÚN CÉITINN (1570–1650)

Will You Be Sensible, Girl!

Will you be sensible, girl!
  And take that hand away;
I'm not the man for the task,
  Be love-sick as you may.

Look how my hair is gray,
  Bodily I'm unfit,
Even my blood runs slow—
  What can you hope from this?

Pray do not think me cruel,
  Oh! do not hang your head,
Of course I will always love
  You, but not in bed.

Let us break up this kiss,
  Tho' it be hard to say,
Let us forbear to touch,
  Warmth to desire gives way.

Your curly, clustered poll,
  Your eyes more green than dew,
Your fair white rounded breasts,
  These are incitements too.

Everything but the one—
  Sharing your body's quilt—
I would do for your love,
  Everything—short of guilt.

translation by Máire Mhac An Tsaoi

ANONYMOUS (18ᵀᴴ–19ᵀᴴ CENTURIES)

If You Come

If you come at all
Come only at night,
Tread ever so warily
And please don't scare me.
Under the door
You'll find the key
And I'll be alone—
Don't frighten me!

No pot in your way
Not a stool or a can
Or a rope of hay
Not a pin, man!
The dog is so tame
He won't bat an eye—
And where's the shame,
I trained him, didn't I?

Mother's asleep
Dad's hands on her hips,
Kissing her mouth,
Her slow-opening lips.
Ah now, it's fine for her!
But my heart is lead—
Lying on my own
In a feathery bed.

translation by Gabriel Rosenstock

ANONYMOUS (18ᵀᴴ–19ᵀᴴ CENTURIES)

Ringleted Youth of My Love

Ringleted youth of my love,
With thy locks bound loosely behind thee,
You passed by the road above,
But you never came in to find me;
Where were the harm for you
If you came for a little to see me,
Your kiss is a wakening dew
Were I ever so ill or so dreamy.

If I had golden store
I would make a nice little boreen,
To lead straight up to his door,
The door of the house of my storeen;
Hoping to God not to miss
The sound of his footfall in it,
I have waited so long for his kiss
That for days I have slept not a minute.

I thought, O my love! you were so—
As the moon is, or sun on a fountain,
And I thought after that you were snow,
The cold snow on top of the mountain;
And I thought after that, you were more
Like God's lamp shining to find me,
Or the bright star of knowledge before,
And the star of knowledge behind me.

You promised me high-heeled shoes,
And satin and silk, my storeen,
And to follow me, never to lose,
Though the ocean were round us roaring.
Like a bush in a gap or a wall
I am now left lonely without thee,
And this house I grow dead of, is all
That I see around or about me.

translation by Douglas Hyde

ANONYMOUS (18ᵀᴴ–19ᵀᴴ CENTURIES)

The Flowering Sloe

(Abridged)

A pleasant lad gave me a present on market day
And after that a hundred kisses—it's no lie I say;
Woe betide the one who says you're not my love;
And I'd court you in the woods as sure as there's a God
    above.

A hundred men would have me when they see me drinking ale
But I recall your words and shiver and grow pale;
The mountain side is whitening with the cold blown snow—
And my darling is as fair as the flowering sloe!

Were I a boatman I would hurry across the main
And were I a poet I would write down all my pain:
A pity the dawn won't see us lying down side by side
In some secluded dewy glen—and nothing to hide!

translation by Gabriel Rosenstock

ANONYMOUS (18ᵀᴴ–19ᵀᴴ CENTURIES)

The Coolin

Have you seen the fair-haired lady walking
Along the roads in the bright dew of the morning?
Many a blue-eyed youth desires her for his own,
But they will not win her love, for she is mine alone.

And have you seen my dear in the late afternoon
Her arms full of flowers and her hair overflowing?
She is the honeyed promise of summer coming soon,
And every idle fellow dreaming she's his own.

Have you seen her at evening, down beside the shore,
Her gold rings sparkling as she braids her hair?
No wonder Captain Power of the Venus once declared
That he'd give his ship to kiss the lips of one so fair.

translation by Michael Slattery

ANONYMOUS (18TH–19TH CENTURIES)

The Brink of the White Rock

Beside the river there dwells a maid,
Of maidens she's the fairest,
Her white neck throws the swan in shade,
Her form and face the rarest.
O she's the maid who my love betrayed,
And left my soul all shaken;
O there's no cure, while life endure,
Since my love has me forsaken.

I'd rather far, than Erin's shore,
Or the Spaniard's golden treasure,
Were you and I in the green woods nigh
To walk there at our leisure.
Or were we wed, dear love instead,
Our parents both consenting;
Sweet maid, your kiss would make my bliss,
If you're to me relenting.

Oh! if you'd freely come with me,
In fashion brave I'd dress thee,
In satin fine your form would shine,
And finest silk caress thee.
Your kine will come each evening home,
Your bees hum in the clover,
Your coach in golden pride shall roll,
When we drive to the white rock over!

translation by Margaret Hannagan and Seamus Clandillon

ANONYMOUS (18ᵀᴴ–19ᵀᴴ CENTURIES)

Small Black Rose

Rose, let go of pain, of all that's happened to you,
The brothers are coming, travelling by sea,
Comfort will come yet from the Pope in Rome
And we won't spare the Spanish wine for my small black Rose.

A long time we've been together, she and I.
We walked many a mountain, crossed many a sea.
I remember leaping the Erne with the water high,
String music on every side was my small black Rose.

God forgive you, your flighty ways are hard on me,
My fate bound into yours a long time now.
Body and soul you have me drained,
Don't let your man down now, my small black Rose.

I'd walk in the morning grass with you, or the bitter desert
For a small part of your heart, your willful love;
My perfumed branch, you swore blind you loved me—
Exquisite flower of Munster, my small black Rose.

If I had the means to, I'd plough the mountain's face,
I'd make my Rose the gospel in the Mass,
I'd have a kiss for the girl giving herself to me,
Happy behind a high ditch with my small black Rose.

The Erne will thunder in flood, the mountains roar,
Salt red the waves will climb, the sky will fill with blood
And every glen in the mountains, every meadow will tremble
Before you'll die on me, my small black Rose.

translation by Theo Dorgan

ANONYMOUS (18ᵀᴴ–19ᵀᴴ CENTURIES)

The Red-Haired Man Reproaches His Wife Who Has Left Him

They are saying your little heel fits snugly in the shoe,
They are saying your lips are thin, and saying they kiss well too;
You might have had many's the man, if what they are saying
  is true,
When you turned your back on your own, but only the tailor
  would do!

I'd have you know, nine months I was tethered in gaol,
Bolts on my ankles and wrists and a thousand locks on the
  chain,
And yet, my flight would be swift as the homeward flight of
  the swan
To spend but a single night with the Wife of the Red-Haired
  Man!

And I thought, "One home we will share, Beloved, for you
  and for me,"
And I thought, "'Tis you will sit there and coax my babe on
  your knee."
Heaven's King's curse be on him who has taken away my
  good name!
So that lies in the end of it all separate us in shame.

translation by Máire Cruise O'Brien

Máirín de Barra

Oh, Máirín de Barra, you have made my mind feeble,
And you've left me sad and lonely, all unknown to my people;
As I lie on my pillow, it's of you I'm always dreaming,
And when I rise in the morning, my heart is still bleeding.

Oh, Máirín, you swept away my sense without warning,
As you knelt in the chapel on Candlemas morning;
Your eyes were far purer than the dewdrops on the barley,
And your voice was far sweeter than the linnet or starling.

I thought I would win you with kisses and coaxing,
I thought you'd be conquered by my promises and boasting;
I was sure that I could charm you as the barley turned golden,
But you left me broken-hearted when the harvest was over.

Oh, happy are the pathways where you stray and you
    saunter,
And happy are the blackbirds with the melodies you've
    taught them;
Oh, happy and thankful are the blankets that warm you,
And how happy for the bridegroom who'll stand beside you
    at the altar.

Oh, Máirín, take my warning, don't let any man cheat you,
Stay away from the tailor and beware of his scheming;
As O'Flynn is my name, I swear I'd never ill-treat you,
Oh, clasp me to your heart, love, you'll have your people's
    agreement.

Oh, Máirín, if you'd have me, I would walk the world proudly,
I'd take you over the water with no thought of a dowry;
I'd leave my friends and my own people, I'd have no fear of
drowning,
For you'd save me from the grave, love, if you placed your arms
    'round me.

Now I'll drink to your health, love, I'll drink it late and early,
And if we were on the sea, love, I'd drink deep as we were
    sailing,
If you'd meet me on the quay, love, there's no fear I'd keep
    you waiting,
And, please God, in a year, love, you could be feeding our
    baby.

translation by Brian O'Rourke

Illustration by Peadar Mc Daid.

136 ∞ LONGING FOR A KISS

THOMAS MOORE (1779–1852)

Did Not
(from *Juvenile Poems*, 1801)

'Twas a new feeling—something more
Than we had dared to own before,
   Which then we hid not:
We saw it in each other's eye,
And wished, in every half-breathed sigh,
To speak, but did not.

She felt my lips impassioned touch—
'Twas the first time I dared so much,
   And yet she chid not;
But whispered o'er my burning brow,
"Oh, do you doubt I love you now,"
Sweet Soul! I did not.

Warmly I felt her bosom thrill,
I prest it closer, closer still,
Though gently bid not,
   Till—oh! the world hath seldom heard
Of lovers, who so nearly erred,
And yet, who did not.

THOMAS MOORE (1779–1852)

The Kiss

Give me, my love, that billing kiss
I taught you one delicious night,
When, turning epicures in bliss,
We tried inventions of delight.

Come, gently steal my lips along,
And let your lips in murmurs move,—
Ah, no!—again—that kiss was wrong—
How can you be so dull, my love?

'Cease, cease!' the blushing girl replied—
And in her milky arms she caught me—
'How can you thus your pupil chide;
You know 'twas in the dark you taught me!'

ANONYMOUS (19ᵀᴴ CENTURY)

Young Lad

Young lad with the curls and the lips made for kissing,
Would to God you and I from our people were missing,
In a tavern at Howth or abroad in the heather,
With gold in our purse, and we wedded together!

I thought, O my love, (I was young and not clever)
That your troth, like a ring, meant you'd part from me never:
You seemed after that like the star in my heaven,
Or the raspberry blossom on the roadside at even!

Would the dark lad and I were where no one could enter,
For nine days and nine nights and from spring until winter,
With iron-bound shutters to fasten our chamber,
And the key in a place not a soul could remember!

How I wish that the dark lad and I were both kneeling
At the altar in church, with the wedding-bells pealing!
If the clergy were late, be sure I and my dearest
Would roam in the sun through the depths of the forest!

Seven weeks by the window a vigil I'm keeping,
As I list to his dreaming and watch him while sleeping;
I'm hiding each kiss with my mantle bent double,
And 'tis love for the rascal has brought me to trouble!

Young lad in whose face the shy sunbeam reposes,
Whose breath is far sweeter than thyme or wild roses,
I never could blame you, your faults I pass over,
Excepting you sleep far too sound for a lover!

translation by Donal O'Sullivan

ANONYMOUS (19TH CENTURY)

The Pearl of the White Breast

There's a colleen fair as May,
For a year and for a day
I have sought by ev'ry way her heart to gain.
There's no art of tongue or eye,
Fond youths with maidens try,
But I've tried with ceaseless sigh yet tried in vain.
If to France or far-off Spain,
She'd cross the wat'ry main,
To see her face again the seas I'd brave.
And if 'tis heav'n's decree,
That mine she may not be,
May the Son of Mary me in mercy save.

Oh, thou blooming milk-white dove,
To whom I've given true love,
Do not ever thus reprove my constancy.
There are maidens would be mine,
With wealth in hand and kine,
If my heart would but incline to turn from thee.
But a kiss, with welcome bland,
And touch of thy fair hand,
Are all that I'd demand wouldst thou not spurn;
For if not mine, dear girl,
Oh, Snowy-breasted Pearl!
May I never from the Fair with life return!

translation by George Petrie

PÁDRAIG PEARSE (1880–1916)

Ideal

Naked I saw thee,
O beauty of beauty!
And I blinded my eyes
For fear I should flinch.

I heard thy music,
O sweetness of sweetness!
And I shut my ears
For fear I should fail.

I kissed thy lips
O sweetness of sweetness!
And I hardened my heart
For fear of my ruin.

I blinded my eyes
And my ears I shut,
I hardened my heart
And my love I quenched.

I turned my back
On the dream I had shaped,
And to this road before me
My face I turned.

I set my face
To the road here before me,
To the work that I see,
To the death that I shall meet.

translated from the Gaelic by Thomas MacDonagh

AUSTIN CLARKE (1896–1974)

Mable Kelly

Lucky the husband
Who puts his hand beneath her head.
   They kiss without scandal
Happiest two near feather-bed.
He sees the tumble of brown hair
Unplait, the breasts, pointed and bare
   When nightdress shows
   From dimple to toe-nail,
All Mable glowing in it, here, there, and everywhere.

Music might listen
   To her least whisper,
Learn every note, for all are true.
   While she is speaking,
   Her voice goes sweetly
To charm the herons in their musing.
Her eyes are modest, blue, their darkness
Small rooms of thought, but when they sparkle
   Upon a feast day,
   Glasses are meeting,
Each raised to Mable Kelly, our toast and darling.

Gone now are many Irish ladies
Who kissed and fondled, their very pet-names
Forgotten, their tibia degraded.
She takes their sky. Her smile is famed.
Her praise is scored by quill and pencil.
   Harp and spinet
   Are in her debt
And when she plays or sings, melody is content.

No man who sees her
   Will feel uneasy.
He goes his way, head high, however tired.
   Lamp loses light
   When placed beside her.
She is the pearl and being all of Ireland
Foot, hand, eye, mouth, breast, thigh, and instep, all that we
      desire.
Tresses that pass small curls as if to touch the ground;
   So many prizes
   Are not divided.
Her beauty is her own and she is not proud.

translation from the Irish

MÁIRE MHAC AN TSAOI (B. 1922)

from The Quatrains of Mary Hogan

Part I
If I could fly this entangled net—
God grant it may be soon!
Memory might come to my aid yet—
How in your arms I'd swoon.

When again I'm able to pray,
Receive Communion and hear Mass,
Who then is to say
It's unseemly what I ask?

Meanwhile listen to this:
Don't get yourself in a knot,
I won't be a slave to your kiss,
I'm giving away what I've got.

translation by Gabriel Rosenstock

Italian Poems

"Francesca da Rimini and Paolo Malatesta" by J.A.D. Ingres, 1819.

DANTE ALIGHIERI (1265–1321)

The Divine Comedy: Canto 5

When I replied, my words began: "Alas,
   how many gentle thoughts, how deep a longing,
   had led them to this agonizing pass!"
Then I addressed my speech again to them,
   and I began: "Francesca, your affliction
   moves me to tears of sorrow and of pity.
But tell me, in the time of gentle sighs,
   with what and in what way did Love allow you
   to recognize your still uncertain longings?"
And she to me: "There is no greater sorrow
   than thinking back upon a happy time
   in misery, and this your teacher knows.
Yet if you long so much to understand
   the first root of our love, then I shall tell
   my tale to you as one who weeps and speaks.
One day, to pass the time away, we read
   of Lancelot, how love had overcome him.
   We were alone, and we suspected nothing.
And time and time again that reading led
   our eyes to meet, and made our faces pale,
   and yet one point alone defeated us.
When we had read how the desired smile
   was kissed by one who was so true a lover,
   this one, who never shall be parted from me,
While all his body trembled, kissed my mouth.
   A Gallehault indeed, that book and he
   who wrote it, too; that day we read no more."
And while one spirit said these words of pitty to me,
   the other wept, so that, because of pity,
   I fainted, as if I had met my death.
And then I fell as a dead body falls.

translated by Allen Mandelbaum

CAMILLO SBARBARO (1888–1967)

Now That You Have Come

Now that you have come,
dancing into
my life
a guest in a closed room—
to welcome you, love longed for so long,
I lack the words, the voice,
and I am happy just in silence by your side.

The chirping that deafens the woods
at dawn, stills
when the sun leaps to the horizon.

But my unrest sought you,
when, as a boy,
on summer nights I came
stifled to the window:
for I didn't know, and it worried my heart.
And yours are all the words
that came, like water brimming over,
unbidden to my lips,
the desert hours, when childishly
my adult lips rose
alone, longing for a kiss . . .

translated by Catherine O'Brien

Jewish Poems

"Birthday" by Marc Chagall, 1915.

Let Him Kiss Me

Let him kiss me with the kisses of his mouth
For thy love is better than wine.
Thine ointments have a goodly fragrance;
Thy name is as ointment poured forth;
Therefore do the maidens love thee.
The king has brought me into his chambers,
We will be glad and rejoice in thee.
We will find thy love more fragrant than wine.
Sincerely do they love thee.
Draw me, we will run after thee.
I am black, but comely,
O ye daughters of Jerusalem,
As the tents of Kedar,
As the curtains of Solomon.
Look not upon me that I am swarthy,
That the sun has tanned me;
My mother's sons were incensed against me.
They made me keeper of the vineyards, but my own vineyard
    have I not kept.
O tell me, thou whom my soul loveth,
Where thou feedest, where thou makest thy flock to rest
    at noon,
For why should I be as one that veileth herself
Beside the flocks of thy companions?
If thou know not, O thou fairest among women,
Go thy way forth by the footsteps of the flock
And feed thy kids, beside the shepherds' tents.
I have compared thee, O my love,
To a steed in Pharaoh's chariots.
Thy cheeks are comely with circlets, thy neck with beads.
We will make thee circlets of gold
With studs of silver.
While the king sat at his table
My spikenard sent forth its fragrance.

My beloved is unto me as a bag of myrrh,
That lies between my breasts.
My beloved is unto me as a cluster of henna
In the vineyards of Ein Gedi.
Behold, thou art fair, my love, behold, thou art fair.
Thine eyes are as doves.
Behold, thou art fair, my beloved, yea pleasant.
Also, our couch is cushioned.
The beams of our house are cedars,
And our panels are cypresses.

MOSES IBN EZRA (1055–1138)

Your Rightful Portion

Caress the breasts of the lovely girl at night,
And kiss the lips of the beautiful girl all day long.
Spurn those who chide you for loving,
Who counsel you to their own advantage.
Heed my words of truth: There is no life
But in the company of beauty's daughters,
Who stole out of Eden to torture the living,
And there is no man living who is not full of desire.
Plunge your heart into pleasures;
Make merry, drink out of wine-skins by the
Riverside to the sound of lyres, doves and swifts.
Dance and rejoice, clap your hands, get drunk,
And knock on the door of the lovely girl!
These are the delights of the world,
Take your part (as did the priests) from
The ram of installation. Always allot yourself
The very portion that was your leaders' due;
Do not stop sipping the moist lips until you hold
Your rightful portion—the breast and the thigh!

JUDAH HALEVI (1085–1140)

Parting

If parting be decreed for the two of us,
Stand yet a moment while I gaze upon thy face . . .
By the life of love, remember the days of thy longing,
As I remember the nights of thy delight.
As thine image passeth into my dreams,
So let me pass, I entreat thee, into thy dreams,
Between me and thee roar the waves of a sea of tears
And I cannot pass over unto thee.
But O, if thy steps should draw nigh to cross—
Then would its waters be divided at the touch of thy foot,
Would that after my death unto mine ears should come
The sound of the golden bells upon thy skirts!
Or shouldst thou be asking how farest thy beloved, I from the
     depths of the tomb
Would ask of thy love and thy welfare
Verily, to the shedding of mine heart's blood
There be witnesses, thy cheeks and thy lips.
How sayeth thou it is not true, since these be my witnesses
For my blood, and that shine hands have shed it?
Why desirest thou my death, whilst I but desire
To add years unto the years of thy life?
Thou, thou dost rob my slumber in the night of my longing,
Would I not give the sleep of mine eyes unto thy eyelids?. . .
Yea, between the bitter and the sweet standeth my heart—
The gall of parting, and the honey of thy kisses.
After thy words have pounded my heart into thin plates,
Thine hands have cut it into shreds.
It is the likeness of rubies over pearls
What time I behold thy lips over thy teeth.
The sun is on thy face and thou spreadest out the night
Over his radiance with the clouds of thy locks.
Fine silk and broidered work are the covering of thy body,
But grace and beauty are the covering of shine eyes.

The adornment of maidens is the work of human hands,
But thou—majesty and sweetness are thine adornment . . .
In the field of the daughters of delight, the sheaves of love
Make obeisance unto thy sheaf . . .
I cannot hear thy voice, but I hear
Upon the secret places of my heart, the sound of thy steps
On the day when thou wilt revive
The victims whom love for thee hath slain—on the day when
    thy dead shall live anew,
Then turn again to my soul to restore it to my body;
    for on the day
Of thy departure, when thou wentest forth, it went out
    after thee.

CHAIM NACHMAN BIALIK

Famished Eyes

These eyes are famished and they plead so long,
These lips are thirsty, clamorous to kiss,
These beauties of desire for dalliance,
These hidden love delights like the Abyss
Know not when sated.

And with carnality, riot of joy,
And with flesh sensual, voluptuous,
From pleasure mountains blessed I am cloyed;
Ah! beauty, could you know the langucrous soul you have
      wearied.

No storm has swept my passions, I was clean,
Till beauty breathed her spirit and defiled
A simple lad, brought pitiless to your feet—
A perfect heart, a crystal mind, a child empty of blossom.

Small moment's boundless happiness was mine,
I blessed the hand that hurt, of sad bliss made,
In that small moment's happy, happy joy
A full world crashed about me—great wealth paid for all
      your flesh!

CHAIM NACHMAN BIALIK

The Golden Peacock

The golden peacock flies away,
Where are you flying, pretty bird?
I fly across the sea.
Please ask my love to write a word,
To write a word to me!
I know your love, and I shall bring
A letter back, to say,
With a thousand kisses, that for spring
He plans the wedding day.

Persian Poem

HAFIZ (C. 1300–1388)

The lips of the one I love are my perpetual pleasure:
The Lord be praised, for my heart's desire is attained.

O Fate, cherish my darling close to your breast:
Present now the golden wine-cup, now the rubies of those lips.

They talk scandal about us, and say we are drunks—
The silly old men, the elders lost in their error.

But we have done penance on the pious man's behalf,
And ask God's pardon for what the religious do.

O my dear, how can I speak of being apart from you?
The eyes know a hundred tears, and the soul has a hundred
    sighs.

I'd not have even an infidel suffer the torment your beauty
    has caused
To the cypress which envies your body, and the moon that's
    outshone by your face.

Desire for your lips has stolen from Hafiz' thought
His evening lectionary, and reciting the Book at dawn.

*translated from the Persian by
Peter Avery and John Heath-Stubbs*

Polish Poems

ADAM MICKIEWICZ (1798–1855)

To D. D.

My little darling, when some merry matter
Makes your voice warble and twitter and coo,
Such is the charm of your lighthearted chatter,
I don't dare miss a sound; and this is why
I don't ask questions, don't even reply,
But listen, listen, and listen to you.

Still, when the words light your face with their fire,
When your cheeks glow from the warmth of your song
With the bright luster that sparks my desire,
Oh, when I see your eyes glitter and glisten,
My lips touch yours, and I no longer listen,
But kiss and kiss, and kiss you all day long.

Odessa, 1825

translated by S. Barańczak and C. Cavanagh

ADAM MICKIEWICZ (1798–1855)

Conversation

My love! what need we have of talk?
Why when I want my feelings to share,
I can't just let my soul to yours declare!
Why must it be crumbled to words
Which before they reach your ears and your heart
Will wither on my lips, and in the air fall apart?

I love you—a hundred times I keep on saying,
But you grieve and start to sting,
Complaining that my love I'm not able
To completely say, state, sing;
And in this weary state I have no doubt
I can't give a sign of life before I give out.

I've tired my lips with such vain misuse;
Now I want to join them to yours in amour's abysses,
And our talk to be only with beating hearts—
And passioned sighs and kisses.
And for hours, days, years thus converse
To the end of this world, and the universe.

translated by M. Lipiński

KAZIMIERZ PRZERWA-TETMAJER (1865–1940)

[I Like It When a Woman . . .]

I like it when a woman swoons in an embrace
When lust's abandonment alters form and face
When she pales and her eyes get covered with mist
And her moist lips part to once again be kissed.

I like it when desire and pleasure give their full vent
And she scratches and digs her fingers in awakening ascent
When her breaths are broken and quick for a while
And she surrenders herself with a faint, dawning smile.

I like that shame which continually does forbid
A woman to admit what her lust has undid
And how desire's force overcomes her, and advances
As she seeks lips, but fears words and glances.

I like all these things—and that special moment
When she lies near me worn out and spent
And my thoughts about her take wing
To that heavenly world love can bring.

Roman Poems

OVID (43 B.C.–A.D. 17)

Elegy V

In summer's heat and mid-time of the day
To rest my limbs upon a bed I lay,
One window shut, the other open stood,
Which gave such light, as twinkles in a wood,
Like twilight glimpse at setting of the sun,
Or night being past, and yet not day begun.
Such light to shamefast maidens must be shown,
Where they must sport, and seem to be unknown.
Then came Corinna in a long loose gown,
Her white neck hid with tresses hanging down:
Resembling fair Semiramis going to bed
Or Layis of a thousand wooers sped.
I snatched her gown, being thin, the harm was small,
Yet strived she to be covered there withal.
And striving thus as one that would be cast,
Betrayed herself, and yielded at the last.
Stark naked as she stood before mine eye,
Not one wen in her body could I spy.
What arms and shoulders did I touch and see,
How apt her breasts were to be pressed by me.
How smooth a belly under her waist saw I?
How large a leg, and what a lusty thigh?
To leave the rest, all liked me passing well,
I clinged her naked body, down she fell,
Judge you the rest, being tired she bade me kiss,
Jove send me more such afternoons as this.

translated from the Latin by Christopher Marlowe

---

cast chaste

PETRONIUS ARBITER (D. A.D. 66)

Doing, a filthy pleasure is, and short;
And done, we straight repent us of the sport:
Let us not then rush blindly on unto it,
Like lustful beasts, that only know to do it:
For lust will languish, and that heat decay.
But thus, thus, keeping endless holiday,
Let us together closely lie and kiss,
There is no labour, nor no shame in this;
This hath pleased, doth please, and long will please; never
Can this decay, but is beginning ever.

translated from the Latin by Ben Jonson

JOANNES SECUNDUS (1512–1536)

The Thirteenth Kiss

Faint from our sweet encounter, love, I lay
panting; my languid fingers play on your neck.
The passion was all consuming, my lips were dry,
I could hardly breathe, I saw death before me.
I saw the waves of Styx roll before my eyes,
I saw old Charon waiting on the far shore,
I was trembling in the bottom of my heart
Until your kisses brought me back to life,
And bid the ferryman to wait no longer
But sail back to the shore without me.

I was wrong, I do not mean without me,
I am but a shade in the land of the living.
The feeble soul that dwells within my body
Is a part of you and will forever strive to
Break away from its fragile abode and flee
To its own place in the company of death.
And were it not for your love, my darling
I would leave limbs to the care of darkness.
Come, let your lips join my lips and let
Us bring our souls together in one breath,
Until, as the passion ebbs and begins to flow
As a single stream of life from two bodies.

JOANNES SECUNDUS (1512–1536)

The Seventeenth Kiss

As the red rosebud unfolds its dewy petals
When night begins to fade into rosy morning,
So do the lips of my lady welcome the day
Bedewed by me with kisses though the night.
As the cherry tree blossoms in white and red
After spring has gone but before summer appears
So do her cheeks appear as the new blossoms
Of snow-white violets held in a virgin's hand.
O miserable me! Your kisses burn my heart,
Why must I be forced to leave your side?
Let those lips remain like roses all day long
When evening brings you to my bed again.
But if another lover should seek your lips,
May your lips grow paler than my cheek.

Russian Poems

YEVGENY BARATYNSKY (1800–1844)

The Kiss

That kiss you gave me, soft and light,
Pursues me in my fancy still.
Through noisy day, through quiet night
I feel your touch, I feel its thrill!

I fall asleep, my eyes I close
And dream of you, and dream of bliss.
Deceptive joy!—the sweet dream goes,
To leave but love and weariness.

translated by Dorian Rottenberg

NIKOLAI YAZYKOV (1803–1846)

Elegy

Blest, who upon night's bed can lie
And fold you in his arms at rest,
With brow in brow and eye on eye,
With lips on lips and breast on breast,
Who with his sudden burning kisses
Your sweet seductive lips can break,
And dark breasts, trembling with blisses,
Now lull to slumber, now awake.
But more blest he, O child of Night,
Who, when love's waking passions rouse,
Looks in your eyes that flame so bright,
Upon the marvel of your brows,
Upon your fresh lips, red and sweet,
Upon your young and raven tresses,
Forgetful of joy's stormy heat
And all the strength that it possesses.

translated by C. M. Bowra

MIKHAIL LERMONTOV (1814–1841)

Farewell

Farewell! Nevermore shall we meet,
we shall never touch hands—so farewell!
Your heart is now free but in none
will it ever be happy to dwell.

One moment together we came:
time eternal is nothing to this.
All senses we suddenly drained,
burned all in the flame of one kiss.

Farewell! And be wise, do not grieve:
our love was so short for regret,
and hard as we found it to part
harder still would it be if we met.

translated by Vladimir Nabokov

Gratitude

I am grateful to you for everything,
For passions' long torments,
For bitterness of tears and poison of kiss,
For vengeance of enemies and slander of friends;
For the passion of my heart, wasted in the desert,
For all with which I have been deceived.
Grant only one wish, that from now on
I will not be grateful to you much longer.

translated by Sergei Zagny

AFANASY FET (1820–1892)

Whispering, timid, softly breathing,
trills the nightingale.
Silver brooklet, lazy weaving,
ripples through the vale.

Flickering visions, gleams of beauty,
fantasies of grace;
Magic changes gone, returning,
light a loving face.

Purple shadows smoothly stealing,
creep across the lawn,
Tears and laughter, sighs and kisses,
and the dawn, the dawn!

translated by Henry S. Drinker

❧ Scottish Poems ❧

"Uncle Toby and the Widow Wadman" by C.R. Leslie.

ROBERT BURNS (1759–1796)

Ae Fond Kiss

Ae fond kiss, and when we sever,—
Ae fareweel, and then—for ever!
Deep in heart-wrung tears I'll pledge thee!
Warring sighs and groans I'll wage thee!

Who shall say that fortune grieves him,
While the star of hope she leaves him?
Me, nae cheerfu' twinkle lights me,—
Dark despair around benights me.

I'll ne'er blame my partial fancy,
Naething could resist my Nancy;
But to see her was to love her—
Love but her, and love for ever.

Had we never lov'd sae kindly—
Had we never lov'd sae blindly—
Never met—or never parted,
We had ne'er been broken-hearted!

Fare-thee-weel, thou first and fairest!
Fare-thee-weel, thou best and dearest!
Thine be ilka joy and treasure,
Peace, Enjoyment, Love, and Pleasure!

Ae fond kiss, and then we sever!
Ae fareweel, alas! for ever!
Deep in heart-wrung tears I'll pledge thee!
Warring sighs and groans I'll wage thee!

ANONYMOUS

The Dart of Love

The dart of love as piercing flies
As the seven-grooved spear to fling;
Brown maiden of the liquid eyes,
Warm as my plaid the love I bring.

The damsel there who sang so sweet,
She in a chair of gold demure,
A silken carpet 'neath her feet,
Myself I blessed her face so pure.

Sweet are the birds beside the sea,
Sweet are the swans upon the mere,
Sweeter my lover's voice to me
When a song she pours in mine ear.

O'er the meadows on a calm day
Sweeter than mavis unto me
My lover's voice, a ho, a hey,
Beautiful maid my love is she.

Sweeter to me her kissing lip
Than the honey and the spruce-tree beer,
Though we twain the mead were to sip
From two glasses together here.

translated from Gaelic

ROBERT LOUIS STEVENSON (1850–1894)

Youth and Love

Once only by the garden gate
   Our lips we joined and parted.
I must fulfil an empty fate
   And travel the uncharted.

Hail and farewell! I must arise,
   Leave here the fatted cattle,
And paint on foreign lands and skies
   My Odyssey of battle.

The untented Kosmos my abode,
   I pass, a wilful stranger:
My mistress still the open road
   And the bright eyes of danger.

Come ill or well, the cross, the crown,
   The rainbow or the thunder,
I fling my soul and body down
   For God to plough them under.

❧ Spanish Poems ❧

"Lovers" by Pablo Picasso.

JARCHAS (11ᵀᴴ–13ᵀᴴ CENTURIES)

Yes, Oh my Lord

Yes, Oh my lord,
Do not kiss
My red lips,
For I shall turn to saffron.

Little Mouth of Pearls

Little mouth of pearls,
Sweet as honey true,
Come, kiss me
My love, come to me, do.

If Thou Desirest Me

If thou desirest me as a tasty morsel,
Kiss this my string of pearls,
Little mouth of cherries!

CHRISTÓBAL DE CASTILLEJO (C. 1490–1550)

To Love

Give me, Love, kisses without end,
Intertwined as hairs on my head,
A thousand and one kisses send;
Then yet a further thousand shed,
And after
Many thousands, another three.
Now, lest some prying eyes should see,
Let us in vain scratch out the score,
And recount backwards, as before.

"Paolo and Francesca" by William Dyce, 1837.

GUSTAVO ALDOFO BÉCQUER (1836–1870)

Rhyme XXIII

For a glance: the world;
For a smile: the heavens;
For a kiss . . . I don't know
What I'd give for a kiss!

Ukrainian Poems

"Irate Drinkers and kissing Couple" by Pieter Bruegel.

LEVKO BOROVYKOVS'KYI (1808–1889)

The Cossack and the Maiden (Parting)

Maiden
My dove of delight! My Cossack so dear!
Will kisses be yours on the steppes wide and drear?
Who'll cover you gently when evening is grey?
Who'll rouse you from sleep at the dawn of the day?

Cossack
Some valley will lull me to rest in my roaming
And thick mists shall cover my form in the gloaming;
The winds and the wild woods will awake me with grace;
In the dew of the fields I shall rinse off my face.

Maiden
O Cossack, my darling! In regions apart
Will you be forgetting your constant sweetheart?
Send news of your fortunes, I ask as a boon . . .
The wish of my heart is: Pray come again soon!

Cossack
My letters with tears shall be written, I swear,
And sent to my love on the wings of the air . . .
Wherever on earth this poor Cossack may roam,
How could he forget you, my darling at home?!
Two stars that shine bright in the dark of the skies
Will always remind me of your hazel eyes;
The raven's black wings will recall your dark hair
That kindled my love into ecstasy rare;
A cranberry bush hints your cheek's crimson rose,
A fir-tree, the grace of my lass as she goes!

Maiden
Your heart to no other give truly, my lad!
And come again soon, that my soul may be glad!

translated by C.H. Andrusyshen and Watson Kirkconnell

PAVLO TYCHYNA (1891–1967)

You Know How the Linden Tree Whispers . . .

You know how the linden tree whispers
In the springtime, at night, by the light of the moon?
    My love sleeps, my love sleeps,
    Let's go and wake her up, kiss her eyes.
    My love sleeps . . .
You heard because of the way the linden tree whispers.

Do you know how the old grove sleeps?
It sees everything, even through the fog.
    Here is the moon, here are the stars, the nightingales . . .
    "I am yours," overheard the old grove.
    And those nightingales . . .
Well! You already know, how the old grove sleeps!

translated by Hélène Turkewicz-Sanko

VITALII KOROTYCH (B. 1936)

Love Her!

The one whom I had no chance to love.
Kiss her,
The one whom I could not kiss.
I'll turn into dust
To fall at her feet.
I'll fly as an owl,
To hoot the song of pain.
I did not have the time
In which women are loved.
I did not know how to kiss,
Smearing the verses with lips.
Near my cradle—a whip.
Over my grave—a tavern.
And around the tiny churches
Haggard mushrooms.
And around me they haggle
Over taverns, over churches, over people.
And around me they sing
Growing deaf of their own clamor.
And she is not there, the beloved.
She is there, in the mob.
But can one hear her—
So tiny, so inarticulate?
Inarticulate lovers.
Whom I could not hear.
Inarticulate poets
Incapable of shouting.
I live in jail.
Near my cradle stands a whip.
My path is marked
By autocrats standing watch.
I don't have a wife,
And I have no sons.

As a heavy emblem
The sun blinks in the puddle.
My progeny, children of black, heavy days,
These are my poems, my songs—lonely and strong.
I am a poet. I am alone.
I am entering into a deadly fray.
I'll die soon—
From lies or from metal.
After long years
The world will see my grandsons,
The sons of my poems, and the women who could have loved me.

translated by Martha Bohachevsky-Chomiak

IVAN DRACH (B. 1936)

A Girl's Fingers

God, the groans there are in fingers,
Cries of anguish in the bluish tips;
In the sultry fingers, the pleasure finders,
In the gentle sufferers, the hands.

God, how much of sweltering shimmer
In those fingers, swaddlers of woe,
Fire-torches of the grafted conscience
With which but my shadow dares be friends.

They shine—o fire-flies, sweet dawns,
World washed by kisses,
Finger-mistresses, lovers, slaves,
In silence toiling, in mute love.

What else can they do, the hundred-tongued
And mute; shine out, and you'll die.
Curse, I curse and chop with a cold blue cry
The dignity of fingers and their brazenness.

Five tiny suns I fall asleep.
Above—the fingers, finger-stars,
Honeysuckle, bitter and so sunny
Penetrates from fingers into me.

translated by Martha Bohachevsky-Chomiak

Love Poetry from Hippocrene Books . . .

CLASSIC AMERICAN LOVE POEMS
The Editors of Hippocrene Books
illustrated by Rosemary Fox
From patriotism, familial and brotherly affection, first romances, and passion—to loss, anguish and tragedy—these verses express a unique American voice on the subject of love. The anthology contains over 100 inspiring love poems from 47 American poets, encompassing works from colonial days to the twentieth century.
135 pages • 6 x 9 • illus. • 0-7818-0645-3 • $17.50hc • (731)

CLASSIC ENGLISH LOVE POEMS
edited by Emile Capouya
This lovely anthology comes in a charming gift edition and contains 87 classic poems of love from 48 poets that have continued to inspire over the years.
130 pages • 6 x 9 • illus. • 0-7818-0572-4 • W • $17.50hc • (671)

CLASSIC FRENCH LOVE POEMS
edited by Lisa Neal
illustrations by Maurice Leloir
This lovely gift edition contains 77 inspiring love poems, translated into English from French, the language of love itself, including a complete translation of Paul Géraldy's *Toi et Moi*. Also featured are 25 beautiful illustrations from famous artist Maurice Leloir.
111 pages • 6 x 9 • illus. • 0-7818-0573-2 • $17.50hc • (672)

SCOTTISH LOVE POEMS: A PERSONAL ANTHOLOGY
Re-issued edition
edited by Lady Antonia Fraser
Lady Fraser collects the loves and passions of her fellow Scots, from Burns to Aileen Campbell Nye, into a book that will find a way to touch everyone's heart.
253 pages • 5½ x 8¼ • 0-7818-0406-X • NA • $14.95pb • (482)

HEBREW LOVE POEMS
edited by David C. Gross
illustrated by Shraga Weil
Several translators have reworked over 90 love lyrics from biblical times to current poetry written in modern Israel.
"A volume of great beauty and range."—*Booklist*
91 pages • 6 x 9 • illus. • 0-7818-0430-2 • $14.95pb • (473)

IRISH LOVE POEMS: DÁNTA GRÁ
edited by Paula Redes
illustrated by Peadar McDaid
Mingling the famous, the infamous, and the unknown into a striking collection, these works span four centuries up to the most modern of poets such as Nuala Ni Dhomhnaill and Brendan Kennelly.
146 pages • 6 x 9 • illus. • 0-7818-0396-9 • W • $17.50hc • (70)

TREASURY OF WEDDING POEMS, QUOTATIONS AND SHORT STORIES
The Editors of Hippocrene Books
illustrated by Rosemary Fox
This beautifully illustrated volume contains over 100 poems, quotations and short stories from over 50 authors—all on the subject of weddings!
150 pages • 6 x 9 • 30 illus. • 0-7818-0636-4 • $17.50hc • (729)

Love Quotations & Proverbs . . .

TREASURY OF LOVE QUOTATIONS FROM MANY LANDS
This charming gift volume contains over 500 quotations from 400 great writers, thinkers and personalities—all on the subject of love. These are words of wit and wisdom from all over the world (over 40 countries and languages), from antiquity to present day. With lovely illustrations throughout, this volume is the perfect gift of love for anyone.
144 pages • 6 x 9 • illus. • 0-7818-0574-0 • W • $17.50hc • (673)

TREASURY OF LOVE PROVERBS FROM MANY LANDS
This anthology includes more than 600 proverbs on love from over 50 languages and cultures, addressing such timeless experiences as first love, unrequited love, jealousy, marriage, flirtation and attraction. Charming illustrations throughout.
146 pages • 6 x 9 • illus. • 0-7818-0563-5 • W • $17.50hc • (698)

All prices subject to change without prior notice. To purchase Hippocrene Books contact your local bookstore, call (718) 454-2366, or write to: HIPPOCRENE BOOKS, 171 Madison Avenue, New York, NY 10016. Please enclose check or money order, adding $5.00 shipping (UPS) for the first book and $.50 for each additional book.